LAST THINGS FIRST

LIBRARY OF LIVING FAITH

JOHN M. MULDER, General Editor

LAST THINGS FIRST

BY

GAYRAUD S. WILMORE

THE WESTMINSTER PRESS
PHILADELPHIA

Scripture quotations from the Revised Standard Version of the Bible are copyrighted 1946, 1952, © 1971, 1973 by the Division of Christian Education of the National Council of the Churches of Christ in the U.S.A., and are used by permission.

BOOK DESIGN BY DOROTHY ALDEN SMITH

First edition

Published by The Westminster Press ®
Philadelphia, Pennsylvania

PRINTED IN THE UNITED STATES OF AMERICA

9 8 7 6 5 4 3 2 1

Lyrics from "When I've Sung My Last Song," by Thomas A. Dorsey, are copyright © 1943 by Thomas A. Dorsey. Copyright Renewed, Assigned to Unichappell Music, Inc. (Rightsong Music, Publisher). International Copyright Secured. All Rights Reserved. Used by permission.

Library of Congress Cataloging in Publication Data

Wilmore, Gayraud S.
Last things first.

(Library of living faith)
Bibliography: p.
1. Eschatology.   I. Title.   II. Series.
BT821.2.W47   236   81-23136
ISBN 0-664-24412-2   AACR2

CONTENTS

FOREWORD

The word "theology" comes from two Greek words—
theos ("God") and *logos* ("word" or "thought"). Theology is simply words about God or thinking about God. But
for many Christians, theology is remote, abstract, baf-
fling, confusing, and boring. They turn it over to the
professionals—the theologians—who can ponder and inquire into the ways of God with the world.

This series, Library of Living Faith, is for those Christians who thought theology wasn't for them. It is a
collection of ten books on crucial doctrines or issues in
the Christian faith today. Each book attempts to show
why our theology—our thoughts about God—matters in
what we do and say as Christians. The series is an
invitation to readers to become theologians themselves—
to reflect on the Bible and on the history of the church
and to find their own ways of understanding the grace of
God in Jesus Christ.

The Library of Living Faith is in the tradition of
another series published by Westminster Press in the
1950s, the Layman's Theological Library. This new collection of volumes tries to serve the church in the
challenges of the closing decades of this century.

The ten books are based on the affirmation of the

7

Letter to the Ephesians (4:4–6): "There is one body and one Spirit, just as you were called to the one hope that belongs to your call, one Lord, one faith, one baptism, one God and Father of us all, who is above all and through all and in all." Each book addresses a particular theme as part of the Christian faith as a whole; each book speaks to the church as a whole. Theology is too important to be left only to the theologians; it is the work and witness of the entire people of God.

But, as Ephesians says, "grace was given to each of us according to the measure of Christ's gift" (Eph. 4:7), and the Library of Living Faith tries to demonstrate the diversity of theology in the church today. Differences, of course, are not unique to American Christianity. One only needs to look at the New Testament and the early church to see how "the measure of Christ's gift" produced disagreement and conflict as well as a rich variety of understandings of Christian faith and discipleship. In the midst of the unity of the faith, there has never been uniformity. The authors in this series have their own points of view, and readers may argue along the way with the authors' interpretations. But each book presents varying points of view and shows what difference it makes to take a particular theological position. Sparks may fly, but the result, we hope, will be a renewed vision of what it means to be a Christian exhibiting in the world today a living faith.

These books are also intended to be a library—a set of books that should be read together. Of course, not everything is included. As the Gospel of John puts it, "There are also many other things which Jesus did; were every one of them to be written I suppose that the world itself could not contain the books that would be written" (John 21:25). Readers should not be content to read just the volume on Jesus Christ or on God or on the Holy Spirit and leave out those on the church or on the Christian life or on Christianity's relationship with other faiths. For we are called to one faith with many parts.

The volumes are also designed to be read by groups of people. Writing may be a lonely task, but the literature of the church was never intended for individuals alone. It is for the entire body of Christ. Through discussion and even debate, the outlines of a living faith can emerge.

"The last will be first, and the first last" (Matt. 20:16). These words of Jesus have puzzled Christians for centuries, but they have also inspired hope and faith. They involve what Christians call eschatology—the doctrine of the end and purpose of human life and history. The theme of eschatology has been particularly prominent in black Christianity, which has given the doctrine a distinctive emphasis. Writing from a black perspective, Gayraud S. Wilmore interprets this idea for all Christians today and shows that it is not simply "pie in the sky when you die" but a source of meaning and mission in the contemporary world. Dr. Wilmore is Martin Luther King, Jr., Memorial Professor and Director of Black Church Studies Program at Colgate Rochester Divinity School/ Bexley Hall/Crozer Theological Seminary. A minister in the United Presbyterian Church, he has been a leader in the quest for social justice for black Americans as the director of the denomination's Council on Church and Race. Through his books and articles he has made a major contribution to the development of black theology.

JOHN M. MULDER

Louisville Presbyterian Theological Seminary
Louisville, Kentucky

1

LIFE, THE BIBLE,
AND JESUS CHRIST

From the beginning of human history people have been fascinated by ultimate questions. What is death, and what, if anything, lies beyond it? What is the future of the world and the destiny of history? The ancient philosophers assigned questions like these to a certain class of theories that had to do with the *telos,* the end or completion of everything that exists or will exist.

The tremendous impact of Greek philosophy upon Judaism and early Christianity made it difficult for thoughtful believers to resist speculation, based upon the Bible, about "the end." Later on, a branch of Christian theology arose called, from the Greek *eschatology,* "the doctrine of last things." Eschatology then became systematic thinking about such topics in Scripture as death, judgment, heaven and hell, and the end of the world.

This book is about such topics. It does not presume to answer all our "eschatological questions"; rather, it intends to explore a few of them. Perhaps the most important consequence of our exploration will be the discovery that what Christians believe about "last things" may be *first* in terms of influence upon their behavior in the world. In any case, let us begin by orienting ourselves in the context of practical life and biblical revelation from

which Christian thought and action receive their most
distinctive characteristics.

Little children can ask the most embarrassing questions—embarrassing to others, but not to themselves.
They have no hang-ups about what their questions may
reveal about themselves—what others may think about
their opinions, or about the family's background, socioeconomic status, or sex life. They are willing to "let it all
hang out," as we used to say in the 1960s.

"Where did I come from, Mom?" What mother has not
had that question thrown at her? Or, "Where did
Grandpa go when he died?"

If we adults do not ask those kinds of questions
anymore, it is not because we have found convincing
answers. It is more likely that we do not want other
adults to know that after twenty or thirty years of maturity
we have not found them, at least not to our deepest
satisfaction. But there is another reason.

For many of us who live in North America during these
last years of the twentieth century such ultimate questions as these have presumably been settled—at one
level of our consciousness—by modern science. Where
did we come from? From amoebas and the primordial
apes. Where will we go when we die? Back into the dirt
that will surround our coffins—where else? Such are the
terse answers of science. But somehow they satisfy only
that one part of our consciousness, the part that has been
shaped by education, the print media, and the local
public television station that regularly shows the popular
scientific specials. In other words, most of us pick up this
kind of information from the ethos of the technological
society in which we Americans live. No matter that in the
pensiveness of our private thoughts or communing with
nature on a quiet walk through the park we may not
really be disposed to trust such ultimate concerns to the
conventional "authorities." But these authorities contin-

ue to provide the most immediate and convenient answers for dealing with those embarrassing questions that children ask and that we have not yet settled in our own hearts.

Somehow the smug answers of science, no matter how verifiable, do not suffice. There is something in most of us that cries out: "But isn't there more? There must be something more about me than amoebas, apes, and cemetery dirt." And so the innocent questions of our children become our questions too, even though we never ask them so innocently as they do. We prefer to mask them in other kinds of grown-up questions.

The black poet Paul Laurence Dunbar was writing not only about his own people but about every adult human being when he said:

> We wear the mask that grins the lies,
> It hides our cheeks and shades our eyes—
> This debt we pay to human guile;
> With torn and bleeding hearts we smile,
> And mouth with myriad subtleties.

Guile. Perhaps that is why Jesus said, "Unless you turn and become like children, you will never enter the kingdom of heaven" (Matt. 18:3). We have to become as children again if we are going to expose ourselves to the mystery of life and death, and to the way the Christian faith seeks to deal with the fundamental questions of our human existence.

FACTS DON'T ALWAYS TELL THE TRUTH

If you have lived long enough, perhaps you have already noticed that facts don't always tell the truth. Facts tell us a great deal about reality, certainly enough to solve an arithmetic problem in our income tax returns, bring a criminal court jury to a decision, or send a space shuttle into orbit. But facts do not always tell us the truth, because: (1) we may not have all the facts, not even the most important ones for what we want to know; (2) we may not put them together in the most illuminating way; (3) we may not understand properly how the facts relate to other important aspects of reality—for example, our humanity, our will to survive, our need to love and be loved.

Item: A divorced mother on welfare pleads with the judge just before her teenage son is sentenced for automobile theft. "Your Honor, I know that the facts prove that Billy stole Mr. Brown's car. But you see, I am Billy's mother and I *know* him. I know that the *truth* is that Billy didn't steal that car. Believe it or not, he really meant to only borrow it!"

Item: The coach of a professional basketball team is interviewed by the hometown press after winning the national championship. "I know we were number one in every department—highest scores, fewest shots, fewest fouls, best defense, and so forth. But, when you look at the facts, I mean a lot of other things besides statistics, the *truth* is, they had the better team. We had the breaks."

Item: The Nazi Gestapo arrives at a house where a young Jewish girl is being harbored in a secret attic. "We have information," says the chief agent to the man who comes to the door, "that she is hiding here." Muller replies, "No, she is not here." The agent scowls and grabs Muller by the collar. "Is that a fact? Don't lie to me!" Muller sighs, "I have told you the *truth.* She is not here!" The agent releases his collar and they move on to the next house.

These little slices of life may make you think about how we communicate with one another. You may have some doubts about whether these incidents prove the point about the ambiguity of facts and how they can be used, but at least they illustrate the problem we all have with truth in real-life situations. Such problems come up in a particular way when we are called upon to answer the questions or deal with the fantasies of little children. What is truth? Children are not the only ones who challenge facts. Who can forget the invisible white rabbit in *Harvey*?

Facts are one thing, but we all know that truth is something else. Children frequently know that better than adults. In real life, facts often deal with the superficial surface of reality. Truth has a way of dealing with the subjective ground of reality. There is something profoundly personal about truth, for in the final analysis it relates to everything significant to our lives. Facts may or may not establish the truth between persons. Truth is greater than facts. And when facts do *violence* to the truth, they no longer reflect what is really going on—or is really true.

There is a kind of fanaticism about facts in a business society where science and technology have sway over judgments of truth and values. The advertisers love to give us the "facts" about consumer goods on the market because they know that the toothpaste sells best that can impress us with the most facts about what it does for cavities and oral hygiene. Our society also *sells* facts. The drugstore bookracks are full of paperback almanacs, encyclopedias, record books, and books of lists. The commercial television channels air nationwide quiz shows all afternoon, and call-in trivia contestants vie with one another on radio. It has become a measure of intelligence whether or not one can remember the first names of Laurel and Hardy or give the name of the singer whose records sold more than a million copies last year. Trivia is the right word for such facts.

Abroad in our land is a mania for facts and more facts. One gets the impression that it does not matter what facts, but how many. The idea is to collect as many as

possible in every conceivable field. Then if you stack
them up in little piles or somehow rearrange them, it is
possible to come up with the truth. That is, perhaps, an
inevitable consequence of living in the age of data banks
and computers when momentous decisions affecting our
lives are made by someone feeding in facts and punching
out answers on an electronic keyboard.

Behind all this madness, of course, is the knowledge
explosion of the late twentieth century. It is impossible
to keep up with the flood of information pouring out of
university laboratories, government bureaus, and research centers all over the world. But how we *evaluate*
what we find out is related to a certain stream of tradition
in Western civilization coming out of Greek philosophy.
The tradition is that rationality is based upon laws rooted
in the natural order and that goods and ends should be
determined by an intellectual process based on the
constant examination of facts.

This philosophical tradition, out of which the modern
scientific process evolved, had certain advantages over
the idea that a Divine Will has absolute jurisdiction over
our judgments about everything, and that the church is
the only authority which can say what that Will demands.
As long as this was the case, human progress toward true
knowledge of persons and things was stymied by an
ecclesiastical oligarchy often more intolerant of the truth
than the most atheistic scientist.

But the liberation of science from the church was not
an unmixed blessing. If the elimination of value judgments based upon subjectivity, superstition, and mysticism made modern scientific objectivity possible, the
new obsession with "scientific facts," which cannot have
anything to do with people's desires and predispositions,
robbed the scientific point of view of something human.
Art, poetry, music, myth, storytelling, inspiration, and
revelation—all of which depend upon intuition, imagina-

tion, and the experience of another reality than that
which can be measured in the laboratory or reduced to a
mathematical equation—became suspiciously unde-
pendable, basically nonfactual, as facts were understood,
and therefore not to be taken seriously as knowledge by
sophisticated people.

Let us not misunderstand what is being said here. It is
not that science should be based on feeling rather than
fact. That would land us right back into ethical arbitrari-
ness or religious authoritarianism. It is, rather, that facts,
like the Sabbath, were made for human life and not
human life for facts. It is too easy to forget that human
values do not come out of a test tube (although test tubes
may sometimes be necessary to establish their verifiability and predictability under controlled conditions), but
values arise from not-so-controllable human decisions
about what is true, right, and fitting for persons in
relationship with other persons. To put it another way,
what really makes living worthwhile is discovering what
it means to be a human being—in the most profound
sense of that word "human."

Of course there are other possible and more apprecia-
tive ways of looking at science, but what is sometimes
called scientism is what we are questioning. The main
point is this: while we all need facts to keep us in touch
with realities that cannot be ignored with impunity,
purely factual data from a dispassionate science which
disregards values cannot give us the wisdom we all need
to live by. We need something else to tell us what facts
are important for human life and why. The values by
which we reckon the humanness of our lives come from
something we call truth rather than fact.

To sum up: facts and values are mutually dependent,
but in a technological society dominated by a crass
materialism it is easy for values to be forced out of the
picture. People, after all, are not laboratory-controlled,

efficiency-rated facts. We are both rational and emotional beings made in the image of the intelligent Power who created us, individually unique and precious "in the sight" of that Power. We are indeed interested in facts! But the fact that interests us most is our humanity. We are not absolutely certain about all that that word means, but we know that it has something to do with faith—with the conviction that we are creatures of God. We yearn to know fully *that* truth which has everything to do with how we live our practical, daily lives—working, playing, loving, trusting, dying.

As Dietrich Bonhoeffer said, "The world has come of age." In such a world Christians must respect facts, but they do not have to be intimidated by them in the search for truth.

The Bible Deals with Truth

This does not mean that there are no facts in the Scriptures or that they do not make any difference. When we read the Bible we learn many facts about the ancient world, particularly about the people of Israel. No one can read about Moses' intemperate violence against an Egyptian, David's dalliance with the wife of Uriah, Jesus' cry of forsakenness from the cross, or Paul's confrontation with Peter at the council in Jerusalem, without the feeling that we are dealing here with factual material about real people. We say to ourselves: "This is no fairy tale. I know these people. I meet them every day."

But the Bible is more interested in communicating with us than in giving us factual biographies or a precisely factual history of the past.

During the 1960s I had a personal acquaintance with the late Dr. Martin Luther King, Jr. Today in my office there are two excellent photographs of him. But there is

also a portrait painted by an exceptionally gifted artist
who has done what only the best photographer could do,
and perhaps more. He has captured on canvas the spirit,
the personality of the man as I knew him. The portrait
communicates something about Dr. King that no photograph I have ever seen conveys.

The Bible is a portrait of life, not a photograph. The
factual details it contains are not unimportant. Scholars
have spent more than two thousand years digging them
out. They have helped us to understand better the
authorship of the various parts of the Scriptures, the
actual conditions under which they were written, the
correct sequence of events, and much more. The significance of the Bible, however, is not in the factual material
but in the wisdom it contains about life, the truth about
what we call the human situation. And that truth has
demonstrated its trustworthiness down through the ages
far beyond anything called factual verifiability.

I once lived next door to a family that never subscribed
to or bought a newspaper. That is strange for highly
educated persons in these days, and they were well
educated. One day I was talking to my neighbor about a
story in the local newspaper. He admitted that he never
felt it was necessary to read a paper. "Why not?" I asked.
"Don't you want to know what's going on in the world?"
"Going on?" he smiled. "When I want to know what is
really going on in the world I read my Bible."

Granted that even the best newspapers give us a
kaleidoscopic and frequently distorted picture of the
world, it is difficult to see how intelligent people can get
along without them. My neighbor's point, nevertheless,
is worth considering. If we want to know the *truth* about
life, the world, and human destiny, we need to read the
Bible, because that is what it is about. Its purpose is not
communiqués of fact but the communication of truth. It

delves beneath the surface of passing events and speaks to us about meaning and consequences. It questions us more than we question it. It enters into a personal dialogue with us not so much about facts as about verities. The greatest theologian of our day, Karl Barth, had the best idea when he said that Christians need both the Bible and the daily newspaper. They should go out into the world with the Bible in one hand and the newspaper in the other, reading one, so to speak, through the other.

Those who look for what someone has called a document of "absolute *verbal* veracity" should not look for it in Scripture. They will find it more likely in the annual report published in Washington by the Secretary of the Treasury, in a surveyor's manual, or in a scientific journal in their physician's office. But don't bet on it! If, on the other hand, you want to explore the contours and pathways of a mountain of wisdom that humankind has accumulated by divine inspiration since the dawn of recorded history, then the Bible is the book to read. There are, of course, other more literal approaches to Scripture that would treat the Bible as scientific fact. In Chapter 3 we will take a look at one such approach.

But now we are saying something quite different. In a way that no textbook or newspaper crammed with flawless detail can, the Scriptures of the Old and New Testaments will lead willing readers, who approach them with humility and an open mind, out of the empirical world of fact and into the vital world of truth. And what they will discover there will be more than information that changes with the times and seasons. Rather, it will be abiding knowledge—the true knowledge of life.

That is why the man who proved the fact of gravity, Sir Isaac Newton, wrote: "No sciences are better attested than the religion of the Bible."

JESUS CHRIST IS THE TRUTH

The abiding *truth* that the Bible reveals and that millions of people have found to make the greatest difference for their lives is the major thrust of the Gospel of John; however, the following passage from The Letter to the Hebrews puts the matter in an interesting way for our purposes:

> In many and various ways God spoke of old to our fathers by the prophets; but in these last days he has spoken to us by a Son, whom he appointed the heir of all things, through whom also he created the world. He reflects the glory of God and bears the very stamp of his nature, upholding the universe by his word of power. (Heb. 1:1-3)

That is certainly not easy to explain to those little children who ask embarrassing questions about the origin and destiny of the human race! It is, nevertheless, where we must begin, and it is the beginning of the kind of wisdom we have been discussing. All of us who are serious about the faith have to make an effort somehow to understand it and teach its meaning to our children.

The Bible contains the words of ordinary men and women through whom God spoke in times past. We can read what they wrote literally or figuratively, depending upon the manner of expression and the context—and, of course, according to our method of interpretation. There are many kinds of literature in the Bible, and anyone who attempts to read them all in one way—as if all were statements of fact or all were poetic rhetoric—is bound to misunderstand the meaning. The writers, after all, were people like ourselves, though gifted in a special way.

People express themselves with words in different ways. Anyone who does not understand the difference between, "We took a trip to New York last week to see a new play," and "That play we saw in New York last week was a real trip!" obviously doesn't understand that the same word can be used to convey many different meanings for different reasons.

"But in these last days he has spoken to us by a Son . . . by his word of power." Jesus Christ comes to us not as words on pages of a book, but as the living Word of God, as one whose life, death, and resurrection sum up all the spoken and written words *about* God in the one Word that *is* God, confronting us "in the likeness of sinful flesh" (Rom. 8:3). We will have to look (all too briefly) at what that means, for it is a matter of great consequence for understanding what this book is about.

Our words are an imitation of life. Whether in prose or poetry, a factual news item or an inspired sonnet, we convey only pictures, symbols, images of life. But if one may revise an old saying for a different time, "Never send a girl to do a woman's job." When something important is at stake, no one wants to use an imitation. Everyone wants the real thing. Instead of using the words of prophets and prophetesses in the Holy Scriptures, God now spoke in the person of Jesus Christ. In that ultimate and perfect way of communicating with human beings God gave the world life itself, not an imitation of life.

> In the beginning was the Word, and the Word was with God, and the Word was God. He was in the beginning with God; all things were made through him, and without him was not anything made that was made. *In him was life, and the life was the light of humankind.* (John 1:1-4, italics added)

JESUS CHRIST IS THE LIFE

All of us yearn for something more than mere existence. Even biological life does not meet our requirements. Few people would choose a vegetable existence under the constant care of others over a quiet and dignified death. We are not looking for what science would define as existence, but what the Scriptures define as life.

That takes us back to the beginning of this chapter. We began by saying that somehow the literal, scientific, objective way of describing reality—as factual as it may be—does not satisfy us, because we want to know a truth that has to do with our lives on another level—where we really feel "at home," where it makes contact with personhood and neighborhood, working and playing, raising a family and pursuing a career, retiring, and dying.

We meet this Word of truth and life who is Jesus of Nazareth first in the written and preached message of the Gospel—words spoken by or about him and written down in Scriptures. Without the Bible we would be ignorant of his ever having lived on earth among us. It is through the written words that *the Word* speaks directly into our hearts and minds by the mediation of the Holy Spirit. Jesus becomes for us, therefore, the Word of Life, because we experience his presence when we believe that he lives in us and shows us the way to live. "In many and various ways," say the Scriptures, "God spoke of old." But now he speaks in a new and living way "by a Son" from whom we have in John's witness this amazing testimony: "I am the way, and the truth, and the life" (John 14:6). That is the ultimate reality of life, which is to say, the eschatological reality.

To speak of Jesus Christ as the eschatological reality here at the end of this chapter is not to indicate that we are preparing to shift from the simple faith of the Bible to metaphysics. It is to introduce the theological language with which we will soon be engaged. The language of eschatology is theological talk about "last things" in the light of "first things." The Word of Life spoken at creation is the Word of Life spoken in the *eschaton*—in the last age. Thus, Rev. 21:6: "I am the Alpha and the Omega, the beginning and the end."

One final comment about this: we speak of our high school or college graduation as commencement. It is an odd word for a day when most people are so relieved that school is over and the pressure is off that it is difficult to think about something else "commencing." But in a profound sense it is a suggestive word for a crucial time of life. The beginning and the end now come together. Commencement is when the mature substance of all we have achieved in the years of preparation is given a new embodiment in the fertile seed of all that we can expect to achieve in the future—fused together in one rite of passage.

Something old is over so that something new can begin. What is over is an anticipation of what has not yet begun. That which is beginning is the fruition of that which has been planted and has now yielded its seed. Commencement is a kind of midpoint when the potential of the beginning merges with the possibilities of the end, so we can look back with thanksgiving and forward with hope.

The resurrection of Christ was a kind of commencement between creation and the end of history. It is the veritable center of history, containing all that was promised and all that will be fulfilled. The creation and the *eschaton*. In his resurrection the past has culminated and the future is authenticated. It was only after the resurrection that the Scripture could speak of Jesus as the Alpha and the Omega. In him creation and redemption were joined together. Faith says, "Because God raised him from the dead I now see that what was intended was life, not death, and it is the ultimate reality of life toward which God is drawing me and all things."

And so we can say that in Christ's resurrected body the history of the past is fulfilled and the future is pregnant with possibility. That is the subject of eschatology and the central issue of this book. We now need to examine the word and the concept more thoroughly. Perhaps that will help us to answer more *truthfully* the questions behind the questions our children and we are asking.

2

WHAT IS ESCHATOLOGY?

One of the reasons some of us have difficulty when we
read the Bible is that we are not always sure what the
words mean, and a dictionary is not always the solution.
The meanings of words also *change* not only with respect
to the same word in different languages—a familiar
problem for scholars translating Scripture from ancient
Hebrew and Greek to modern languages—but within a
single culture.

We generally think of the United States as a single
culture, but we live in a pluralistic society where words
carry different shades of meaning, depending upon many
factors. Even though one may speak English, if he or she
were not born and raised in a black community and had
not experienced firsthand what it is like to be black in
America, such a person would miss many nuances of
what is being said among street corner men in a Harlem
bar, or even the conversation at a middle-class cocktail
party in Atlanta or in Reston, Virginia. The same thing, of
course, could be said about other kinds of situations
involving ethnic, class, or geographical differences. Not
only do words have a certain flexibility in different
grammatical contexts, they have different shades of
meaning in different social contexts—and even those
meanings change over time.

Take the word "family," for example. When our country was mostly a frontier, family meant kinsfolk, especially in rural areas. Grandmother, grandfather, Mom and Dad, uncles, aunts, and cousins. And often as not, all of these might be found in a single household on a farm or plantation.

Then thirty years ago demographers began to talk about "an urban family of four" and sociologists about "the nuclear family"—mother, father, and two or three children living hundreds of miles away from grandparents and other relatives. Today when the person we used to call the truant officer has to get in touch with the family to see why Johnny is not showing up for school, he or she does not know what to expect. There were 6,000,000 single-parent families in the United States in 1980. Divorced couples often speak of family because even though Mom and Dad are not living together they may be seeing each other regularly, or the children may be shifting from one bedroom to another across the town on an agreed-upon schedule. Some children have identical sets of toys in each house or apartment! Then again, an unmarried couple may qualify as family even though one partner or the other may exchange places with someone else every two or three years. Only the children are stuck with the same address. Two women or two men living together these days, with or without children, will sometimes claim to be a family. Finally, the extended family still exists in many urban as well as rural areas. Increasingly this is true where young people (but also retired persons!) have moved together in communes. Everybody in the house is "family."

We just have to broaden the meaning of family today and we do not get out of it by simply saying, "Let's agree on what family *ought* to mean." That is not as simple as it sounds. What is the most healthy form of human cohabitation under any given set of circumstances? Few thoughtful persons would jump to any hasty conclusions about that. Any pastor knows that the announcement of a church "family night" may hurt someone's feelings. In any event, we can never be too sure about who is going to turn up.

"Sexuality" is another word that has certainly demonstrated flexibility in recent years. To use it used to be considered almost naughty. When we spoke of the sexuality of a man or woman it was assumed that we were talking about something that had mainly to do with a bed. One rarely raised the question of sexuality in polite company without the risk of being misunderstood or at least being regarded as avant-garde.

Today people feel much more comfortable with the word because its connotation has broadened considerably. Sexuality has relevance for a whole range of human relations. Newspapers, magazines, and public television have helped. Most people today will agree that there is almost nothing that concerns our getting along with each other that does not have something to do with human sexuality. So the word is bandied about everywhere—from public school classrooms, to YWCA group therapy sessions, to church covered-dish suppers. Perceptions and understandings have changed with the culture.

Something of the same thing that has happened to change the meaning of family and sexuality has happened to words like gay, soul, chauvinism, evangelical, charismatic, ideology, Negro, and hundreds of other words. Some have narrowed in their generally accepted meaning. Others have broadened. Some are in a state of utter confusion as the transition is being made from one connotation to another. In times that are relatively stable, words that belong to the fundamental realities of life keep their familiar meanings for a long time. But in times of rapid social change like ours most areas of life are fluid and the vocabularies that apply to them change almost daily.

In the field of Christian theology something similar has happened to the word "eschatology." Formerly our images were of death, Christ descending on a cloud to judge the earth, the joys of heaven and the tortures of hell. Today the word has much broader meanings and connotations. Let us see what they are.

Eschatology is still a branch of systematic theology. The word is formed by two Greek words—*eschata*, meaning "last things," and *logos*, meaning "science." If you wanted to be literal about it, you could say that eschatology is the science of the last things, or the science that explains the end of the world. For reasons that will become apparent later we will speak of it as the "understanding" of ultimate realities that have to do with time, history, and human life.

THE HISTORICAL BACKGROUND

Most religions and philosophies have been greatly interested in what happens when the present order of existence comes to an end or when an individual dies. Early Greek and Roman religions had a concept of an underworld where the dead were judged and existed in cycles of a thousand years. The Stoic philosophers were concerned with eschatology. When the writer of II Peter talked about the world being destroyed by fire he was probably influenced by mystical Stoic eschatology (II Peter 3:10). The whole ancient world, including the nation of Israel, was obsessed with the idea of the end of the world and the possibility of life after death. We know that the prophets of the Old Testament looked for the end to come with the appearance of a Messiah who would destroy the enemies of God and bring in a glorious age of peace, power, and prosperity. It is not surprising, therefore, that eschatological thought among the early Christians included the idea of a Final Coming of Jesus, the Messiah. The New Testament, from the Gospels to Revelation, reflects the eschatology of the Old Testament and particularly of the intertestamental period shortly before the birth of Christ. Eschatology did not begin with John writing the book of Revelation on the island of Patmos.

Great questions such as the origin and destiny of the universe, time and eternity, the reward of goodness and punishment of sin, were subjects of weighty argument and speculation by the theologians of the church during the first five centuries after Christ. Irenaeus, a bishop of Lyons in the second century; Clement and Origen, who belonged to the influential Alexandrian school of theology in the third century; Tertullian of North Africa; and the greatest of all, Augustine (354-430), a native of Tagaste in Numidia, North Africa, and bishop of Hippo— all knew pagan as well as Jewish eschatology. Even though they resisted heretical speculations about "the last things," based upon non-Christian sources in Africa and the eastern Mediterranean world, their interpretations of Christian eschatology could not avoid being influenced by them. Even more important is the fact that those same influences played upon the writers of the Gospels and Revelation.

All of this is to say that when we talk about eschatology in the old way, we have a mixture of Jewish prophecy, pagan mythology, and Greek religious and philosophical speculation. The eschatological sections of our Bible did not fall down one day from heaven, pure and unadulterated, into the minds of those who shaped the orthodox faith of the early church. This does not mean, of course, that we can dismiss what they wrote as prescientific rationalizations in face of the awesome mystery of death and an unknown future. The German scholar Albert Schweitzer proved conclusively in the 1930s that the self-understanding and ministry of Jesus were saturated with eschatological thinking, and eschatology is crucial for an understanding of the Christian faith.

What this means is that, in the light of what we now know about the way the Bible was written and the essence of the faith of the primitive church, we ought to proceed carefully. The word "eschatology" has a broader and deeper meaning today than it had fifty years ago. That meaning is related to the present as well as the future. It is also related to what we were saying in the first chapter about facts and truth—making distinctions between a literal reading of Scripture and one that takes into due account the historical development of ideas and the changing meaning of words. Eschatology still deals with what one Sunday school pupil called "that spooky stuff in the Bible," but what it really means and how it can be applied to our life today has radically changed, at least for some believers.

THE THEOLOGICAL DEBATE

At the end of the nineteenth century Christians who wanted to take seriously the scientific picture of the world attempted to de-emphasize the eschatological passages of the Bible. Whether we speak of the resurrection, the empty tomb, Christ returning to earth riding on a cloud, the gathering before the great white throne of God for the Final Judgment, the joys of heaven and the fires of hell—none of these, so they argued, is essential to an understanding of who Jesus was and what he wants us to be and do in these modern times. What is really important is the ethical teachings of Jesus—to acknowledge God as our Father, men and women as our brothers and sisters, and to love our neighbor as ourselves. That is what the religion of Jesus was about. The rest is obsolete—first-century theatrics—the set and the background music.

A book by Johannes Weiss, *Jesus' Preaching on the Kingdom of God*, published in German in 1892, and two books by Albert Schweitzer, *The Mystery of the Kingdom of God* (English translation, 1925) and *The Quest of the Historical Jesus* (English translation, 1910), took issue with this point of view. Weiss and Schweitzer demolished the idea that Jesus and the New Testament writers had something else in mind and that their eschatological bias could be ignored. Using the exegetical tools of the best scholarship, they were able to make a convincing case for the commanding role that eschatology plays in the New Testament. Jesus meant precisely what he said. And when the writers of the New Testament speak of last things in terms of a catastrophic end to history and the visible return of Christ they are not simply providing background music for his timeless ethical teachings—they are presenting what Jesus actually believed himself and what the early church expected momentarily. This different way of looking at the message of Jesus and the New Testament challenged both the traditional and the liberal picture of his life and ministry in the respect that it made the eschatological expectation the consistently controlling factor. Accordingly, this view has been called *consistent* eschatology, meaning an eschatological understanding of the religion of Jesus unadulterated by modernizing qualifications and revisions.

Once the attempt of liberal scholars to portray Jesus as a nineteenth-century man had been exploded by Weiss and Schweitzer eschatology was liberated from the blind faith of orthodoxy and the modish acculturation of their contemporaries. The doctrine of the last things was then opened for further interpretations supporting or refuting the work of the German scholars.

Charles H. Dodd (1884-1973), the great British New Testament scholar, popularized a new position in the

1930s called *realized* eschatology. Dodd argued that the Kingdom which Jesus preached and the eschatological events accompanying it had already been realized or fulfilled in his life and ministry. Instead of projecting the last things into the future—events to occur at the end of history—realized eschatology held that the supernatural had entered into history with Jesus. It agreed with Schweitzer's position that the New Testament is thoroughly eschatological, but disagreed that Jesus was referring to something that he mistakenly believed would come only in his lifetime or in the near future. The future, said Dodd, was inaugurated with the preaching of the Kingdom of God and everything that was available for Jesus and the disciples is now available for those who accept the eternal life which Christ came to bring.

Realized eschatology made the promises of the Old Testament and the new life of which the New Testament speaks available here and now. It satisfied the need of many liberal Christians to make the gospel contemporary and not leave everything to some obscure and remote future. The time was indeed fulfilled and the eschatological judgment and blessing had somehow begun and were present in the world of our experience. But realized eschatology, some said, did not deal satisfactorily with the idea of the Final Coming. That event, at least, seemed clearly in the future. The problem of biblical eschatology had not been entirely solved.

By emphasizing the fulfillment of prophecies of the end during the earthly life of Jesus, realized eschatology was grounded in the events of that time although with meaning for modern Christians.

A third form of eschatology in the theology of Karl Barth has been called *transcendental* eschatology because in this view the final truth about our life and the life of the world, rather than expected in a future history or realized in a past history, exists in every age in a

transcendent, timeless realm above history. It is, in other
words, an eternal truth available at all times—past, present, and future—to those who have faith in Jesus Christ,
the Word of God. We do not have to look back into the
past or forward into the future to grasp eschatological
reality. It exists in an eternal Now. Like a stationary
communications satellite it is forever near to and forever
distant from the points on the earth above which it
hovers—equally accessible to all receivers that are tuned
to receive its messages. Barth was not impressed so much
by the *last* things as he was by the *eternal* things.

The theology of Rudolf Bultmann, Barth's contemporary, has given us yet another theory of the last things
which we may call an *existential* eschatology. Combin-
ing the insights of those who preceded him, Bultmann, in
an article entitled "The New Testament and Mythology"
(1961), discussed biblical eschatology in the context of
his concept of demythologization which means reinter-
preting mythic elements of the biblical story so that the
essential core of the apostolic preaching produces something of deeply personal significance for the life of the
hearer—not facts for knowledge, but truth for subjective
existence, not history as a record of chronological events,
but history as the unfolding of human experience that
opens up momentous possibilities for the subjective
choices and decisions one must make in order to be fully
human.

When this way of thinking (or rather, of being or
existing!) is applied to the problem of eschatology the
New Testament references to the last things are reinterpreted as if they relate, in a different way than Dodd
understood, to the present experience of the believer. *I*
experience a shock of recognition by which the eschatological teaching becomes transparent to *me*. And far from
dissolving the mythic elements of eschatology, my awak-
ened consciousness uses those very elements to lay hold

upon truth which, at this time and under these circumstances, could not have been grasped in any other way. The New Testament, from this perspective, gives me a truth not so much timeless as timely—a truth that has to do with more than the literal meaning of the text, cloaked in its mythological vesture, but with the immediate world in which my personal existence is at stake.

NEWER THEOLOGICAL PERSPECTIVES

These, in brief and without doing justice to their full complexity, were the four major ways eschatology was understood before Jürgen Moltmann's *The Theology of Hope* was published in 1965. Moltmann was not satisfied with making eschatology the tail of theology—the last chapter after everything else of importance had been disposed of. Like Schweitzer, he objected to making it a kind of appendix that could be removed without disturbing any of the vital organs of systematic theology. On the contrary, Moltmann's theology placed the eschatological hope at the center of Christian thought—radiating out to the distant horizon of faith and doctrine. His eschatology encompasses everything in its view. Thus, to think theologically is to think eschatologically, and the foundation of Christian thought is not reason or understanding, but hope.

Although he gave Schweitzer credit for opening up biblical eschatology for serious consideration in modern times, Moltmann went beyond him. He also felt that Barth and Bultmann had obscured "the real language of eschatology" by employing modes of thought from the ancient Greek philosophers rather than from the thought forms of the Jewish prophets. In his view transcendental and existential eschatologies make the final truth about human life exist either in the great, eternal Beyond or the great, eternal Within. Both depend upon classical philo-

sophical ideas about ultimate reality. They are essentially metaphysical and, therefore, miss the point that biblical eschatology is not a science of what is or what ought
to be. Rather, it is an anticipation of what does not yet
exist at all but is hoped for against every reasonable
possibility that it could ever be.

Moltmann turned the discussion of eschatology back
from objective revelation on the one hand and existential
subjectivity on the other, to human history, to social,
political, and economic realities in the process of transformation by Christian hope and action. In the preface to
one of his recent books, *The Church in the Power of the
Spirit* (1977), Moltmann tells us what are the implications of his theology of hope for ecclesiology—the doctrine of the church:

> Because hope means the power of life, and life is lived in
> open relationships, the kingdom of God ought not to be
> described in abstract terms. It must be seen concretely, in
> all the living relationships in which Christianity is in-
> volved. The future of the church is only described through
> the medium of a church of hope for other people and with
> other people.

This is important, because one of the major characteristics of the current discussion of eschatology is the attempt to spell out its relevance for the unity and mission
of the church in the modern world. Although Moltmann
does not consider his work a part of the movement of
liberation theology, he has been greatly influenced by
this new school of theology which arose in the black
community of the United States and in Latin America in
the 1960s. The quotation above illustrates how his eschatology takes on political relevance in response to the
prevalence of injustice and revolution in the world today.
Like other contemporary Protestant and Roman Catholic
theologians on the continent of Europe, where socialism
offers a more popular alternative to capitalism than in the

United States, Moltmann sees the Church Militant as an eschatological community which translates its hope of the Kingdom of God into the kind of political activity that can change the world.

The proponents of liberation theology—James H. Cone, a black American scholar, Gustavo Gutiérrez of Peru, Juan Luis Segundo of Uruguay, and others—are more specific about what those changes should be. They seem more clearly to emphasize the political character of eschatological hope in a socialist revolution of the have-nots of the world against the haves. There is, in any case, a more explicit theme of economic class or racial struggle in the Christian-Marxist orientation of the liberation theologians than in the political theology of Moltmann and American theologians who also are concerned about human liberation, such as Paul Lehmann, Schubert Ogden, and Rosemary Ruether. Undoubtedly the two groups of contemporary theologians—one mainly from the Third World and the other from the First World—have learned from each other. Both call for a demonstration of the world-transforming power of the Christian faith and make the vision of a better society the central theme of their theologies.

The black American liberation theologian James H. Cone sees eschatology in terms of the struggle against all forms of oppression, but especially racial oppression in the United States. In *A Black Theology of Liberation* (1970), Cone writes:

> Black Theology does not scorn Christian hope; it affirms it. It believes that, when people really believe in the resurrection of Christ and take seriously the promise revealed through him, they cannot be satisfied with the present world as it is. . . . As long as we look at the resurrection of Christ and the expected "end," we cannot reconcile ourselves to the things of the present that contradict his presence. It is this eschatological emphasis that Black Theology affirms.

Yet the structure of the ideal society of the future is more vague in black theology than in the liberation theology of the Latin Americans. Cone and other black theologians are clearer about what ought *not* to exist than they are about what *should* exist. But it is more evident in black theology today than in most of the works of white American theologians that some form of socialism based on a Marxist analysis of history is closer to Utopia than anything that the mainstream American political parties represent.

Gutiérrez and other Latin Americans do not hesitate to identify the gains of the socialist revolution with the *growth* of the eschatological Kingdom of God, if not with its final consummation. Socialism has saving meaning to them although they are careful to say that it is not *all* that Christian salvation must mean. Liberating praxis (reflective activity on the political and economic front) is a part of what brings in the Kingdom. Juan Luis Segundo speaks of this bringing in the Kingdom as its "causality" and in his writings this work of "bringing in" is closely connected with the consummation of the Kingdom itself. He writes:

> The causality is partial, fragile, often distorted and in need of re-working; but it is a far cry from being nothing more than an anticipation, outline, or analogy of the kingdom. We are definitely not talking about the latter when we are talking about such option as racial segregation versus a truly balanced marketing process, and capitalism versus socialism.

We can see from all that has been said above that eschatology no longer has to do merely with death and dying, heaven and hell. The meaning of the word has been updated to fit the realities of our contemporary world in which a new emphasis is being placed upon human potential in psychological terms and human liberation in racial, economic, and political terms.

Eschatology now applies specifically to what Christians mean by personal existence and cosmic history and what can be experienced in the former and expected from the latter. But the older ideas about last things which are more closely tied to the biblical picture of catastrophe and judgment cannot be dismissed and we must now turn to other ways Christians read the Bible.

The point of this chapter is not only that the debate about eschatology has not been settled among theologians of the mainline churches. It is to say that eschatology is becoming an even more critical issue during these closing years of the twentieth century.

3

PROPHETS, SEERS
AND RACKETEERS

At 9:00 P.M. on May 26, 1981, a group of sixty members of an apocalyptic sect called Yahweh Yohoshua went home disappointed after waiting for the Messiah for several hours on Coney Island Beach in eighty-degree heat. Clad in white headdresses and robes and led by a man they call Apostle Shad Ben Yah, the group began to walk into the surf at 3:00 P.M. when the expected Savior was to appear and part the waters to receive them. The apostle beckoned the waiting congregation to follow, while a large gathering of families and friends tried to persuade them not to commit suicide. After some hesitation the apostle returned dejectedly to the beach.

In an interview with the press, Police Captain William Baer said that he had been contacted by telephone two weeks earlier by someone who warned him that "they would be prepared to leave this earth and go to heaven" on Tuesday, May 26. Fearing an incident similar to what happened at Jonestown, Guyana, on November 18, 1978, New York City policemen were on hand to keep the sect, part of a 500-member congregation, under surveillance.

This strange incident is only the most recent of a long series of predictions of the coming of a Messiah and the end of the world. Thousands, perhaps millions of members of prophet-led sects and cults have known bitter

40

disappointment when it did not happen according to schedule.

The stories of miscalculations stretch over the two thousand years of Christian history and testify to human yearning for divine deliverance. Various terms with different shades of meaning are used to describe eschatological expectations—Messianism, adventism, millenarianism, millennialism, chiliasm, etc. The common element is a belief that focuses almost exclusively on "the last things"—the anticipation of and preparation for a cosmic cataclysm that will bring the world order to a close and usher in the reign of Christ on earth.

APOCALYPTIC AND DISPENSATIONALISM

The term "apocalyptic" describes the highly imaginative and symbolic form in which eschatological hopes are expressed in the Bible and then decoded and elaborated by every generation, including our own. Here are a few of the many texts of biblical apocalyptic that have fired the imaginations of believers, impostors, and unclassified types in between.

> On that day the LORD will punish
>   the host of heaven, in heaven,
>   and the kings of the earth, on the
>   earth.
> They will be gathered together
>   as prisoners in a pit;
> they will be shut up in a prison,
>   and after many days they will be pun-
>   ished.   (Isa. 24:21-22)

Blessed is he who waits and comes to the thousand three hundred and thirty-five days. But go your way till the end; and you shall rest, and shall stand in your allotted place at the end of the days. (Dan. 12:12-13)

But when you see the desolating sacrilege set up where it ought not to be (let the reader understand), then let those

who are in Judea flee to the mountains; let him who is on
the housetop not go down, nor enter his house, to take
anything away; and let him who is in the field not turn back
to take his mantle. And alas for those who are with child
and for those who give suck in those days! Pray that it may
not happen in winter. (Mark 13:14-18)

For the trumpet will sound, and the dead will be raised
imperishable, and we shall be changed. (I Cor. 15:52)

And he seized the dragon, that ancient serpent, who is the
Devil and Satan, and bound him for a thousand years, and
threw him into the pit, and shut it and sealed it over him,
that he should deceive the nations no more, till the thousand years were ended. After that he must be loosed for a
little while. (Rev. 20:2-3)

We can see from these difficult passages that the
essence of apocalyptic is symbolism. The language of
some apocalyptic literature is lurid and intensely imaginative. Fantastic images rise up to veil the writer's
meaning, as if he were speaking only to those who have
the key to unlock the secret message contained in his
words. And that is frequently what happened.

The apocalyptic outlook is usually pessimistic and
negative about the present and sees life ending in a great
cosmic catastrophe. But a positive note is present. God's
people, who endure to the end, will be delivered from
their suffering and persecution when God comes to
destroy the power of Satan.

When will that great event take place? Although Jesus
warned us not to worry ourselves about when the end
would come, Christians have been unable to resist the
temptation to speculate. Those who have either worked
it out in some detail, or are at least persuaded that they
know the various stages of history which precede the
end, are called dispensationalists.

Dispensationalism is an attempt to synthesize or inte-
grate what the Bible as a whole asserts or implies about
history in order to come up with a system of periods or

stages of God's dealings with creation. The assumption is that God dispenses favor and disfavor in a predetermined, systematic way. There is, for example, the dispensation of law which applies to Israel and the dispensation of grace which applies mainly to the church. Dispensationalists refuse to mix the two together, making, for example, the church the spiritual Israel. Not all Old Testament prophecies about Israel have been fulfilled, and the dispensationalists look for fulfillment in the future—perhaps during the thousand-year reign of Christ when the Jewish nation will be restored in Jerusalem. Thus, most welcomed the conquest of Palestine by modern Israel as preparation for what had been promised only to God's chosen people.

Some dispensationalists, like Cyrus I. Scofield (1843-1921), the editor of the famous Scofield Reference Bible, believe in as many as seven dispensations or periodic covenants between God and his creation.

1. Innocence: the covenant with Adam.
2. Conscience: the covenant with Adam after the Fall.
3. Human Government: the covenant with Noah.
4. Promise: the covenant with Abraham.
5. Law: the covenant with Moses.
6. Grace: the covenant through Christ.
7. The Kingdom of Heaven: the restoration of the Davidic monarchy by Christ during his thousand-year reign.

Dividing up history in this way by using the literal meaning of biblical texts or by the manipulation of various sets of numbers which appear in apocalyptic literature permits one to make a stab at the exact time of the end, the great battle called Armageddon (Rev. 16:16), and the thousand-year rule of Christ on earth. In the 1830s, William Miller, a New York farmer who led a movement of thousands of adventists, reasoned that the number 2,300 in Dan. 8:14 meant 2,300 years, and by

working with other biblical dates and numbers he came
to the conclusion that the Lord would return to earth on
October 22, 1844. Obviously, such mathematical systems
present problems, and some people wonder whether it
makes any sense to reduce much more decisive aspects
of Christian faith to such inexact computation.

Dispensationalists are literalists—most of the time. All
of the prophecies of the Bible either have been fulfilled
as written or will be fulfilled in the future. The fact,
however, that dispensationalists disagree about the number of periods, the chronology of eschatological events,
and which passages should be interpreted literally and
which spiritually, raises some questions about the valid-
ity of their method. The principle of dispensational
interpretation is that even if the Bible contains symbols
and figures of speech—such as in the apocalyptic texts
above—one must always search for the literal meaning
behind what is written. Many nondispensationalists
agree that such a search is necessary if the trustworthiness of Scripture is to be upheld. But the problems do not
disappear. Even granting that there is always a literal
meaning (something not everyone is willing to grant) that
meaning is not always plain. The result is great disagreement among dispensationalists, all of whom claim to read
the Bible literally.

E. Mansell Pattison, in *Religious Movements in Contemporary America* (1974), edited by Irving I. Zaretsky
and Mark P. Leone, observes how bitter the debate over
the millennium has become among fundamentalists. Pattison is a psychiatrist who has done research on the
personality orientation of fundamentalists. He believes
that their fierce arguments about the millennium are
basically emotional. Because, the fundamentalist ego
needs to be at war with the world and is unsupported by
the present culture, says Pattison, ego gratification is
emotionally tied to the future. Thus the debate over the

millennium becomes more a question of personal survival than theological argumentation. It becomes a "fight for
life."

Whether or not Pattison's psychological interpretation
is correct it is certainly true that opposing views about
the millennium are the cause of bitter controversy and
internal divisions among the fundamentalist churches.

What Is Millennialism?

The key texts for millennialism are found in the
twentieth chapter of the book of Revelation. Christ will
bind Satan and rule with his saints for a thousand years.
The prophecies in vs. 4-5 have been greatly studied by
scholars, who argue whether they refer to two different
resurrections or one, two deaths or one, the precise
nature of these events, and in what order they will come.
The bottom line is a general attitude or conviction about
the Bible as a whole. If each verse is literally true, then it
follows that a serious reader will want to use every tool of
grammatical and historical research into the original
languages in an exhaustive search for an indisputable
meaning. On the other hand, a somewhat more open-
ended attitude about the nature of biblical material will
yield a less doctrinaire interpretation. And there are
many shades of differences between these two positions.

Three basic positions are referred to within the general
scheme of millennialism.

1. Postmillennialism

Postmillennialism originated after Christianity became the religion of the Roman Empire and includes the
approach of most scholars of the mainline liberal denominations. The millennium does not necessarily mean a
thousand years. It could be more or less and, in any case,

it has already begun. Christ will return *after* its completion. In the meantime the church must preach the gospel
to all nations and help to extend the Kingdom of which it
is a foretaste. Postmillennialism is optimistic about this
mission and the gradual unfolding of God's purposes in
the world. All evidences to the contrary notwithstanding,
the world is really getting better because Christ rules—
even if his rule is hidden from the eyes of unbelievers.
When all things are ready he will come again. Then what
is symbolically presented to us in apocalyptic, say some
postmillennialists, will somehow go into effect in ways
that we cannot be absolutely sure about today.

2. *Amillennialism*

Amillennialism is of more recent vintage. The amillen-
nialists discount the necessity of one thousand years or
any other time period before or after the Final Coming.
What is important is that Christ will come again—without the necessary evangelization and betterment of the
world by the activity of Christians. His coming will be
marked by an immediate resurrection of the dead and the
Final Judgment. Actually the eschatology of amillennialism is open-ended. Since it takes Revelation 20 as mainly
symbolic, it is like postmillennialism, because it can
assume either a period of peace or one of great tribulation. The main point is that if a millennium seems
necessary in order for those who have died in Christ to
be raised, to share judgment and rulership before the
general resurrection (Rev. 20:5), our interpretation of the
Bible does not oblige us to expect one. This position
rests upon a study of the words used in Rev. 20:4-5.
Accordingly, the souls of the righteous have survived in
Christ. They are already "resurrected." And when Christ
comes, resurrection, rule, and judgment will have already taken place in a spiritual sense. Those who are in

Christ will live with him forever. Those who died without the faith will never live again.

Amillennialism is more interested in an exact but nonliteral interpretation of Scripture than postmillennialism, but it comes up with an interpretation that makes it unnecessary to believe in an extended period for the earthly manifestation of the victory of the Lord and his church.

3. Premillennialism

Premillennialism dominated the eschatology of the early church, but it diminished as the Parousia, or Final Coming, was delayed and the church became almost indistinguishable from the Roman Empire. It enjoyed a revival in the nineteenth century as a key doctrine of Protestant revivalism. Today it is most popular among the Holiness and Pentecostal churches. As world conditions worsen in an age of inflation, revolution, and the threat of atomic holocaust, more and more Christians in the mainline denominations expect a premillennial return of Christ.

Premillennialists believe that the Scriptures must be interpreted literally. There is, they contend, no way of escaping the biblical evidence that Christ will return to earth *before* the thousand years of peace. Premillennialism and various forms of dispensationalism go well together because a clear difference is made between the stages of history before and after the physical return of the Messiah. All prophecies must be literally fulfilled and that can happen, with respect to the nation of Israel, only if Christ reigns as the early king of the Jews in Jerusalem before Satan is loosed for the last time.

This eschatology, unlike that of postmillennialism, is starkly pessimistic. Anyone can see, it is argued, that the world continues in its downward moral spiral since the

time of Adam. All the frantic social action of the churches
to make it better is a waste of energy. We are doomed to a
cataclysmic explosion of wickedness. Wars, famines,
earthquakes, and great tribulation for the church will
precede the coming of the Messiah, just as predicted in
the New Testament (Matt. 24; Mark 13; Luke 21) and
passages about the coming Day of the Lord in the Old
Testament.

Only after these events will Christ descend with a
shout and trumpet blast to snatch his true church into the
upper air, along with those saints who will experience
the "first resurrection," to remain with him in what is
called "the rapture." Meanwhile, the final agonies dev-
astate the earth.

Actually "rapture" is not a biblical term and premillennialists differ about this stratospheric suspension of the
saints. Those who believe that Christ will remove his
church *prior* to the devastation are called pretribulation
or "rapture" premillennialists. Those who find no evidence that the church will escape the troubles of the last
days are called posttribulationists. They expect the living
church and the sainted dead to be caught up to meet the
Lord in the *midst* of the tribulation, and return victori-
ously to earth with him. Only then will come the thousand years of peace, followed by the release of the devil,
the final great battle, the second resurrection, the Last
Judgment, and the eternal lake of fire in which Satan and
the ungodly will suffer unimaginable torment forever.

CASHING IN ON MILLENNIAL FEARS

It goes without saying that this scenario has terrified
people for countless generations. While it has sometimes
provoked Christians to revolt against the oppression of
an alleged Antichrist, it has also been the source of no
little mischief. Impostors have used the catastrophe

eschatology of extreme millennial fundamentalism to exploit the naive and defraud the gullible. The leaders of cults and sects obsessed with the imminent destruction of the world and demanding absolute subordination—including the surrender of sex, money, and worldly possessions—have been involved in scandal since false prophets deceived the exiles "for handfuls of barley and for pieces of bread" (Ezek. 13:19).

Sharp bargainers looking for a quick killing encouraged the followers of the Adventist prophetess, Mrs. Ellen G. White, to sell or give away their properties in 1844 when William Miller predicted that the world would end.

Joseph Jeffers of the Temple of Yahweh in Los Angeles taught the approach of an atomic Armageddon and that he was receiving messages about the rapture of his followers from the headquarters of God in the constellation of Orion. In 1945 Jeffers was sentenced to a federal penitentiary for theft, was paroled, and later returned to prison for a similar offense.

The apocalyptic Alamo Christian Foundation, one of the many Jesus People sects, preached repentance and the impending return of Christ from their Hollywood commune in 1964. Daniel Cohen, in *The New Believers: Young Religion in America* (1975), writes about the leaders Tony (formerly Bernard Hoffman) and Susie Alamo:

> Both Tony and Susie dress well and Tony is often described as a flashy dresser. Susie, who was compared with Lana Turner in her acting days, still tries to keep up the old image. The pair also live well when compared with the austere conditions that prevail at the foundation.

Tony Alamo was involved in rock music and boasted his own recording label. "I had the Twenty Original Hits," he once said, "twenty smash hits on one album,

Oldies but Goodies for $2.98. I made loads of money. I was making more than General Motors."

Rev. Sun Myung Moon, leader of the Unification Church, whose assets, estimated in the millions, have been connected with radical anticommunist business interests in Korea, has his own unique eschatology. *The New York Times* reported that his estate in Tarrytown, New York, was worth $850,000. Moon purchased another property for the Unification Church from the Christian Brothers for a reported $625,000. A postmillennial dispensationalist, Moon calls his church a revolutionary movement to establish the Kingdom of God on earth. In an interview with Frederick Sontag on February 3, 1977, he said:

> The Second Coming was predicted because the mission (of Jesus) was not totally accomplished in the first. Therefore, a messianic crusade is destined to begin here on earth in order to consummate the will of God. The work of the Unification Church and my mission is to proclaim the coming Messianic Age.

After numerous charges of brainwashing youthful followers and months of legal battles, the United States Government was seeking Moon's deportation as an illegal alien in June 1981.

These charges of fraud and misrepresentation among some charismatic leaders do not mean to imply that millennialism and the fundamentalism which undergirds it produces movements that are innately more evil than other forms of faith. The perversion of Christianity happens in all sectors of the church. There is no theological dividing line separating the saints from the sinners. But it is not difficult to understand that when the faithful are frightened or mesmerized by eschatological indoctrination, money and power become great temptations to their leaders.

READING THE BIBLE AND BEING THE CHURCH

What shall we make of all this? First, it is clear, as the fundamentalist denominations are wont to remind us, that a literal or nonliteral reading of the Scriptures makes all the difference.

Secondly, even if you choose to read the apocalyptic passages as stylized and imaginative symbols with a deeper meaning, you still have to decide what is *that* meaning. If, for example, Jesus' prophecies of tribulation have already been fulfilled in some spiritual way, and if Revelation 20 was written to strengthen a particular church under persecution, there may be some ultimate significance to struggle and suffering that the mainline denominations have not well understood. For if secularized, middle-class Christianity is anything—it is comfortable. Can even a postmillennialist position that takes the Scriptures seriously, if not literally, be so well adjusted to the status quo? The premillennialists, at least, recognize the hopelessness of secularism and the urgency of warning everyone "to flee the wrath to come."

Finally, we must make up our minds about the role of the church in all of this—the nature of its mission. Whatever may be our interpretation of the eschatological passages of the Bible, the ethical mandates of the gospel remain. What about the poor, the prisoners, the blind, and the oppressed, those to whom Jesus said he was sent, and those who were so passionately defended by the great prophets of the Old Testament? Does the power of sin and the imminent return of Christ imply that works of righteousness in the economic and political fields are contrary to the eschatological plan of the Scriptures? Should the church separate itself from the fallen world, reaching in only to snatch souls from the burning to come? What should be the posture and mission of the church in the modern world as it waits for the return of its Lord?

In Chapter 2 we saw that such questions lie at the heart of the contemporary discussion of eschatology. In a hopeless situation one New Testament writer called upon Christians always to be ready "to account for the hope" that is within them (I Peter 3:15). This Christian hope arises out of the contradiction and forlornness within our own souls and in the world described by apocalyptic. But it is not what we see that we hope for, but "we hope for what we do not see" (Rom. 8:25). It is, therefore, a positive, transforming hope that should impel the church into the future. It is that hope to which we turn in the next chapter.

4

THY KINGDOM COME

In this chapter we are going to shift our attention from contemporary ideas about eschatology to consideration of a particular perspective that many Christians, in the early years of the church and in our own day, have found convincing. This is not to avoid the argument we have been tracing in our previous investigation of different approaches to eschatology. For later in this chapter it will be necessary to look at a somewhat opposing, or at least balancing, viewpoint and its implications for the mission of the church. Then we shall see whether the two perspectives are really one when they are brought together in a mutually corrective way.

Allan D. Galloway, in his book *The Cosmic Christ* (1951), makes a statement that could well serve as the theme of one basic aspect of Christian eschatology—the paradox of the Kingdom of God.

> Something has entered our experience which breaks through the structure of "It," revealing its ground in that to which we can say only "Thou." That is to say, once we have encountered God in Christ we must encounter God in all things. This is the sense in which the Kingdom has already come, and the power of the demonic is already broken in Christ, even though the course of cosmic history has not been violated by any cataclysmic intrusion of the Divine. . . . Yet while the course of history remains thus

unviolated, its entire face, both before and after Christ, has been altered by His presence and His work in the world.

In what sense does he mean that the Kingdom has arrived on earth while we yet continue to pray, "Thy kingdom come"? It is significant that in the prayer that we have learned from Jesus the first petition is that the Kingdom, or reign, of God should become present and effective in the world. If the coming of the Kingdom is the first thing that Christians should pray for, it is a reasonable conclusion that it also occupies the highest priority in what we should hope for. But that is not all. Our hope seems uniquely realistic, because in some sense the Kingdom has already begun.

JESUS CAME PREACHING THE KINGDOM

In the beginning of his ministry, following the arrest of John the Baptist, Jesus came into Galilee with the astonishing message (in Mark's Gospel) that the Kingdom of God was at hand and that his hearers should repent of their sin and believe the good news. He was, in effect, saying that an unprecedented state of mundane existence was now occurring in human history. Jesus understood himself fully in relation to this new situation. He was anointed by the Spirit of God to proclaim the fulfillment of the time of preparation and the opening of the door of God's favor for those who were ready to accept his Lordship and enter into an exceptional relationship with him and with one another.

The signs of this new state of affairs were evident. It was not something that people had to conjure up in their imaginations or think themselves into. It was not "accentuating the positive and eliminating the negative." The empirical evidences of the Kingdom were plain for all to see. Jesus said to the disciples of John, when they came to inquire if he were indeed the promised Messiah who would bring in the Kingdom, or someone else:

> Go and tell John what you hear and see: the blind receive their sight and the lame walk, the lepers are cleansed and the deaf hear, and the dead are raised up, and the poor have good news preached to them. And blessed is he who takes no offense at me. (Matt. 11:4-6)

The early ministry of Jesus, attested by such signs, inaugurated the eschatological Kingdom. "If it is by the finger of God that I cast out demons, then the kingdom of God has come upon you" (Luke 11:20).

Inauguration, however, means a commencement. It makes us anticipate what is to follow. It opens up the present for the future. The *inaugural* nature of Jesus' ministry is understood when we look at its selectivity and localism. Not everyone sick was healed or cleansed of demons. And his miracles did not occur everywhere in Palestine, much less the world. This was only the first signal that something new was beginning—something that would become more spectacular and universal in the future. "Truly, truly, I say to you, he who believes in me will also do the works that I do; and greater works than these will he do, because I go to the Father" (John 14:12). The *eschatological* nature of the Kingdom is understood when we look at how it is precisely opposite to what existed prior to its inception. Jesus reversed the reality he encountered by turning it, so to speak, on its head. The blind *see*. The lame *walk*. The lepers are *cleansed*. The direction in which the inauguration points is toward the end, toward the wholeness of human life and the fulfillment of God's promise—toward the eschatological future that was already breaking in and revealing the amazing new creation that accompanies its perfect actualization in the future.

We speak, therefore, of the presence of the Kingdom,

but at the same time of its coming in the future. Because
it is not yet here we hope for it, but to hope for it means
that in some sense we are already living under its power
which impels us to "make it real."

WHERE IS THE KINGDOM OF GOD TODAY?

That is the question everyone asks. Jack Kerouac, the
beat generation novelist, once said, "I want God to show
me his face." That is like saying, "I want to see this
Kingdom that you claim has already begun." No one
looking out at the world in which we live today—a world
of war, disease, poverty, and violence—can simply on the
basis of positive thinking make a reasonable verification
of the reality of the Kingdom of God. We need to be very
clear that positive thinking is a psychological manipulation of perception to make the world appear to be what
we would like it to be. Sometimes it screws up our
courage and makes us perform more efficiently. Sometimes it doesn't. It is, in the final analysis, a mirror game,
and anyone who plays it is in danger of falling into a ditch
that was really there all the time. But Christian hope in
the Kingdom has nothing to do with the mirrors of
positive thinking. It looks reality in the face unblinking-
ly—without being intimidated by it. Hope accepts what
is, because of its expectation of what will be. Martin
Buber once wrote: "If we only love the real world that
will not let itself be extinguished, really in its horror, if
only we venture to surround it with the arms of our spirit,
our hands will meet hands that grip them."

Because of our faith in the resurrection of Jesus, we
can affirm that the Kingdom he announced and demonstrated nineteen hundred years ago in Palestine was
really the beginning of a new creation which is hidden
within and beneath the sorry mess that we now see all

around us. This means that the Kingdom is not some kind
of realm of perfection—some transcendent reality that
exists somehow above or outside of the world that we
experience every day. It is not some kind of never-never
land in a fairy tale that we imagine to be opposite the
fleshly, material stuff of life that we all have to deal
with—the heavenly over the earthly, the unconditional
in opposition to the conditional. The Kingdom is mixed
up in the real world as a partial and unfulfilled potential
of its being. It is visible in the sense of being a constitu-
ent of that which we see and not something out of sight.
But it is invisible in the sense that it is not yet the
organizing principle of worldly existence, not yet as
effectual as it will be. Because of the resurrection we
have hope that the God who raised Jesus from the dead
will also bring into full view that Kingdom which the
ministry of Jesus introduced. Christian hope refuses,
therefore, to play with those mirrors we were talking
about—making the present look like the future by coun-
terfeit or, in imitation of a skillful card shark, substituting
what is on the table with a marked deck. Christian hope
peers into the mystery of the future with expectation and
deals the cards that are already there, with the assurance
that a winning combination, though difficult to come by,
is somewhere in our hands.

What makes the difference is our present experience of
the risen Christ and our faith that the resurrection is
antithetical to and contradicts the death that all of us
must experience, in the same sense that the perfection of
the Kingdom contradicts the imperfect world we live in.
Furthermore, this same relationship of antithesis and
contradiction applies to the problem of sin. For it is
through the cross and the resurrection of Jesus Christ
that even the sin that we continue to commit is canceled
out.

In the resurrection God reversed reality by turning it on its head, but it continues to be reality, in the sense that the reversal was not done with mirrors or by some sleight of hand. What was there before is still there, but totally and perfectly transformed into the wholeness it lacked before. This is why the Scriptures speak of a "bodily resurrection," though not to be taken as crassly physical. We cannot pierce the mystery of that transformation which made it possible for the risen Lord suddenly to appear before the disciples behind closed doors and say to Thomas, "Put your finger here, and see my hands; and put out your hand, and place it in my side; do not be faithless, but believing" (John 20:26-27). But what this incident tells us about the nature of God's transforming power is that it does not do violence to his creation. It does not insult or despise what he gave to us and in which he sustains us. Rather, it perfects and fulfills the real world by releasing the eschatological potential which lies hidden beneath its surface.

The new creation is really *new*. But it does not exist in some kind of different place inaccessible to our humanity. It is new, but it fills the same space and takes over the identity and function of the old in the sense that in every way it is the true domicile of humanity, a humanity that will itself be changed, taken up in Christ, but not expunged. "And when I go and prepare a place for you, I will come again and will take you to myself, that where I am you may be also" (John 14:3). A "place" is prepared that can accommodate our humanity in its wholeness, and the Lord who invites us there is not a disembodied spirit, but someone to whom we can relate as friend to friend. That is why black congregations love to sing, "What a Friend We Have in Jesus." The journey and friendship into which Jesus summons us begins right here where we first met and followed him.

Thus, the Kingdom is in our midst (Luke 17:21). It is present, even though its fullness is ahead of us in a new future. But only because of the resurrection and the living presence of Christ through the Holy Spirit can we say this. Because of the resurrection we have faith that the world in which we live, despite all its corruption, is filled with the power of the Kingdom of God. The light of that present and coming Kingdom falls upon the world from a distance in the future and lights up both the creation's pockmarks, under the impact of history, and its potential for a flawless complexion. The Kingdom is in the midst of the fallen world in both judgment and grace. This is why the apostle Paul could write that both we and the whole creation "groan inwardly as we wait for adoption as sons and daughters, the redemption of our bodies" (Rom. 8:23). In this hope of the redemption of the physical and material world, of becoming what we are, of the new which redeems the old—"we were saved" (Rom. 8:24).

THE VIEW FROM THE KINGDOM

From this perspective some Christians are able to look upon the world with new eyes. The social, economic, and political structures that order our lives, justly and unjustly, the ecological environment that sustains us in abundance and scarcity, are not devoid of the signs which Jesus called to the attention of John's disciples. By preaching his good news and doing the works of his love, we uncover the reality of his Kingdom, present and coming.

But there are others who see it differently. To share their perspective we must turn to that other side we spoke about in the beginning of this discussion. It may be helpful for us to listen to those who accuse us of using binoculars rather than mirrors to see what we want to

see. Binoculars make what is distant appear to be decep-
tively near at hand. It is possible to become so enrap-
tured before "the rapture" that we assume that the part of
the world in which we live—where the church is still in
business and everything has a slight Judeo-Christian
aroma—is almost heaven. This is a special temptation for
American Christians. And if the world seems to slip a
little from the pedestal we have erected for it, liberals
prop it up with Christian social services and social action
programs which deal with surface imperfections rather
than the rot underneath.

Jacques Ellul in his *The Presence of the Kingdom*
(1951) has this to say about the danger of glossing over
the real situation:

> "Colour-wash the devil in gold, dress him up in white, and
> perhaps he will become an angel!" It is this effort to paint a
> different picture, which all Christian ethics or sociologies
> or politics, or even social Christianity, offer us as a solution.
> ... What people are really trying to do in all these move-
> ments, is to see to it that the condition of the world is not
> *too* shocking for the Christian conscience. In reality men
> are trying to make a bridge between the world and the
> Kingdom of God, and the Christian would find himself
> always upon the bridge!

Ellul has always been suspicious of any eschatology
that relaxes the tension between the Kingdom of God
and this world. Nor does he believe in trying to make a
bad situation more tolerable by the work of do-gooders.
This only serves to disguise the fact that to live in the
world is to live in a den of liars and thieves, in the
domain of Satan himself. It can neither be made less
sinful, nor accepted for what it is. In this uncomfortable
dilemma there is little room for the utopianism of "social
Christianity." Once the church understands and honestly
faces reality the laity will be helped to adopt a certain
style of Christian life that demonstrates faith, not in some

worldly political or economic system, but in the noncon-
forming ethics of the Kingdom of God.

Today many conservative Christians would agree that
this way of viewing the world and the church's responsibility is an important corrective to our earlier position.
On the basis of their alleged dependence upon the Word
of God they see a sharp difference between the world
and the Kingdom. The latter is more to be anticipated in
the future than celebrated in the present. But times are
changing and some of the so-called "new evangelicals"
are willing to grapple with the powers of evil on the
economic and political front. This has been particularly
true of black evangelicals, such as James Forbes and
William Bentley, who, under the influence of black
liberation theology, have declared their independence
from white conservative evangelicals.

Where is the line drawn? In one of the many parables
of the Kingdom the servant asks his master why it is that
since he sowed only good seed in his field weeds are
growing up around them. The reply is, "An enemy has
done this." "Then," asks the servant, "shall we go in and
root out the weeds?" "No," says the master, "lest in
gathering the weeds you root up the wheat along with
them. Let them grow up together. And when the harvest
comes I will then tell the reapers to gather the weeds and
burn them but to gather the wheat into my barn." (Matt.
13:24-30.)

There are some new evangelicals who would say that
in order for the Kingdom to be effective in the present
world the weeds must be rooted out because it is the very
nature of weeds to choke out good grain. Most, however,
would not go so far. There is a way, they would say, to
confront the powers of this age by a "holy conduct and
godliness" (II Peter 3:11) that translates into effective
politics without secularizing the mission.

CAN THE TWO VIEWS BE SYNTHESIZED?

This is a problem for Christian laity who want to be politically active, but also want to avoid the simplistic strategies of the Moral Majority which impose religious solutions where secular solutions would be more appropriate. It may be possible, however, to bring the politics of the world and the politics of the Kingdom together so that the resources of our faith can really make genuine secular decisions without falling into the trap of believing that human action alone can somehow keep the world from reaping the consequences of the evil it continues, despite our best efforts, to sow.

For the more conservative Christian, the idea that we are living in the Kingdom of God, which can use the sinful world to overcome sin, is much too positive a way to view a negative situation. That is, they say, no better than the illusory positive thinking of the religious revival of the 1950s.

For the more liberal Christian, to say that the church is so holy and the world so sinful that the twain cannot meet until the Kingdom comes in some remote, catastrophic future is too negative a way to view a world that still belongs to a sovereign and gracious God.

Perhaps the late Joseph A. Johnson, Jr., one of the leading black theologians of the last decade, helps us to resolve the issue. Johnson maintained that it is precisely the transcendence of the Kingdom that places it in the center of down-to-earth realities. The Christian can render, therefore, an uncompromising obedience—not mournfully, but with shouts of victory, upraised hands, and clapping for joy. In his book *Proclamation Theology* (1977), Johnson wrote:

> The negative point that God's kingdom is sheer miracle must be held fast in stark negativity. This negative which

sees God's kingdom as the quite other, entirely supernatural and antisecular, is much the most positive statement
that could be possibly made. The realization of God's
sovereignty is future. And this future confronts man in the
present.

He goes on to say that when we respond to this
supernatural sovereignty with the kind of obedient faith
that "lets go and lets God," then the Kingdom comes
without much effort and without our being able to take
credit for it. Such is the mystery of grace and the amazing
good news of the gospel.

Liberals may not be entirely comfortable with the
supernaturalism and the emphasis on "letting go," and
conservatives may not be happy with what Johnson
meant by "obedient faith" in view of his lifetime of
staunch opposition to their political and social policies.
But it may be that this way of being Christian begins to
resolve our problem and cannot be labeled either liberal
or conservative, at least not as those terms are used in the
current debate. Perhaps August Meier's classification of
Dr. Martin Luther King, Jr., as "a conservative militant"
comes closest to an accurate description of the major
stream of black religion that both Johnson and King
represented. One can speak of it as a peculiar brand of
evangelical radicalism which is related to the experience
of what W. E. B. Du Bois called the Negro's "twoness—
two warring ideals in one dark body" within American
society.

In any case, it is not a stance that is impossible for
those who are not black to take, but a pointer to something that may be quite universal in authentic Christianity—the reconciliation of power and powerlessness. Historic black faith, born in slavery and climaxing in the
ministry of Dr. King, may have something to say to all of
us about struggle and relinquishment, works of righ-

teousness and justification by grace, hopes that are temporal and the hope that is eschatological. Is it possible
that the synthesis worked out in the black religious
experience can—with some adaptations for the majority
situation—help to close the gap between conservative
and liberal Christianity in our generation?

Let us explore that possibility further in the next
chapter.

5

ANOTHER ESCHATOLOGICAL PEOPLE

Sometime between A. D. 130 and 140, very early in the life of the Christian church, there appeared in Rome a document that was to have great influence among Christians in the second and third centuries. It was called The Shepherd and was written by Hermas, an apostolic father (regarded as having been one of the disciples of the apostles) whose brother was probably bishop of Rome during that period.

The importance of this document for our purposes is that here we have in an early writing which almost made the canon of the New Testament a strong emphasis upon Christian behavior in the world as well as eschatology. It is evidence that as the hope for the early return of Christ faded, church leaders began to reformulate the eschatological hope in terms of its implications for the continuing life of the community in a world that was apparently going on for some time to come.

The Shepherd is difficult to understand because it is composed of visions, parables, and obscure references such as one finds in the book of Revelation. But it seems clear that one intention of the writer was to bring together the ritual of baptism—symbolizing the forgiveness of sins and induction into the church—and the hope of the Kingdom. Hermas puts his emphasis on the call to

holiness and obedience that will be validated by the
future society of the Kingdom of God. A New Testament
writer's letter, written only some seventy years earlier,
makes a similar but somewhat different connection for
those who must have expected Christ's return almost
immediately. Believers are to be different from others, to
live pure lives, to "love one another earnestly," for they
are God's elect.

> But you are a chosen race, a royal priesthood, a holy nation,
> God's own people, that you may declare the wonderful
> deeds of him who called you out of darkness into his
> marvelous light. Once you were no people but now you are
> God's people; once you had not received mercy but now
> you have received mercy. (I Peter 2:9-10)

In The Shepherd of Hermas, however, the discussion
of baptism suggests not only election and priesthood but
ministry to the world. As the period between Christ's
resurrection and Final Coming lengthened and generations of believers experienced the disappointment of its
delay, the apostolic fathers in Rome began to link up the
eschatological expectation with the call for an out-reach-
ing concern for the world. Ray C. Petry comments upon
this second-century document of Hermas (*Christian Eschatology and Social Thought,* 1956):

> Not only is there a marked tendency to look forward to the
> future society of God's kingdom; there is also a clear
> premium placed upon dedication to that kingdom in terms
> of service to the present world society.

During those relatively early years of the development
of the church as an institution the formula that gained
ascendancy went something like this: Christian baptism
and entrance into the church represents membership in a
covenant community that is the New Israel of God;
baptism is inauguration into a life of holiness and service
to the world for the sake and in anticipation of God's
coming Kingdom. The older eschatological attitude that

we find in such a passage as I Cor. 7:20-24—where one is called upon to stay where one is, to remain in the same social status and occupation—is being replaced by a settled attitude of involvement in the world in the spirit of holiness and philanthropy.

The important point is that this was not an abandonment of an earlier eschatological perspective. It was, rather, the adaptation of the older perspective to a new situation, a situation in which it is understood that God's will is for his chosen people to perform works of love and mercy while they tarry for the Parousia. They are admonished, as Hermas reminded them, "that you, as the servants of God, are living in a strange country, for your city is far from this city." For that reason they should take more seriously what Jesus said about being the salt of the earth, the light of the world, a city set on a hill (Matt. 5:13-14). Far from giving up the hope of the Kingdom, they have become an eschatological people in an even more practical sense, because overarching and controlling their daily activity in the church and the world is the vision of that Kingdom—the city "whose builder and maker is God" (Heb. 11:10).

We may think of an eschatological people as one in whom the hope of the Kingdom to come provides the motivating power for living as though it had already come or will come soon by dint of moral effort. Eschatology, in other words, dominates and regulates the self-understanding and behavior of an eschatological community.

There are two basic ways in which an eschatological community deals with the present world in which Christ's coming is delayed. (1) It can withdraw. This means it attempts to deal with the present by hardening the community against its heartaches and disappointments. By coming apart from the world and surrounding the community with an aura of mysticism and transcen-

dence it is possible for such people to experience something of the Kingdom in the moral rectitude and emotional intensity of their life together. (2) It can attack. This
means it attempts to remake the present in the image of
the future; to bring the transcendence of the future
Kingdom into the present by transforming the world that
surrounds the community.

Between these two basic strategies of passivity and
aggressiveness are intermediate positions that combine
elements of one or the other according to the situation in
which believers find themselves at any given point in
history. In any case, an eschatological people or community is consciously motivated by its vision of the end and
that vision is so powerful that it will not be denied some
intentional materialization in the present.

History has produced many communities of both types
in Christianity and in other religions. But it was the
Protestant Reformation of the sixteenth to the eighteenth
century, when there was a "revolution of rising expectations" among submerged classes and natural science
became uncoupled from ecclesiastical control, that
opened the floodgates of millennial dreams and utopian
schemes. The most significant of these communities
were those which sought aggressively to change the
world around them and make the Kingdom of God
visible in the New World across the seas that was now
wide open for exploration and exploitation.

Leonard I. Sweet reminds us that even Christopher
Columbus, in his little-known *Book of Prophecies,*
thought of himself as a "Christ bearer" who would bring
the gospel to infidels throughout the world as a prelude
to the millennium. "God," he wrote, "made me the
messenger of the new heaven and the new earth, of
which he spoke in the Apocalypse by St. John, after
having spoken it by the mouth of Isaiah; and He showed
me the spot where to find it."

THE PURITANS OF NEW ENGLAND

When the English Protestants landed at Plymouth Rock in 1620 and a larger and better organized wave, ten years later, established the Massachusetts Bay colony, they brought with them the sense of being an eschatological people. God had removed them from England to New England—"the place," wrote one Puritan migrant to Boston, "where the Lord will create a new heaven and a new earth in new churches and a new commonwealth together." This sentiment resounds throughout the literature of both Protestant and Roman Catholic settlers of the New World, but nowhere with more fervor, piety, and erudition than in the sermons of the Puritan divines who were immersed in the history of the Old Testament. More than any other immigrants to America they saw themselves as God's New Israel under the second dispensation of grace—an eschatological people in quest of the New Jerusalem. These Puritans well understood the message behind the apocalyptic of The Shepherd of Hermas. For them too the imminent return of Christ had been transmuted into a calling to practice holiness, to do the works of righteousness among the "poor natives (who) before we came were not called by the Lord's name." To build the Kingdom of God in this wilderness as his covenant people.

It goes without saying that the "poor natives" were unimpressed by this concern for their welfare, since thousands were violently dispossessed of their lands and enslaved. Emanuel Downing in a letter to John Winthrop in 1645 speculated that "if the Lord should deliver them into our hands, wee might easily have woemen and children to exchange for Moores (African slaves), which wilbe more gaynefull pilladge for us than wee conceive."

Nevertheless, the Puritans sincerely believed that they had been singled out above all the other peoples of the world to perform great deeds for the Lord in accordance with a covenant theory that was, says the American historian Perry Miller, "the intelligible medium between the absolute and undecipherable mystery of God's original purposes and His ultimate performance, between the beginning and the end of time."

In the next century, Jonathan Edwards, America's first prominent theologian, helped to make the vision of the millennium the cornerstone of mainline revivalism. The eighteenth-century revival of religion known as the First Great Awakening which Edwards helped to start reinforced the contention of William Bradford and John Winthrop that America was destined not only to purify the Church of England but to become the center of the Kingdom of God. Edwards' eschatological writings added a touch of nation-building to revivalism by emphasizing the establishment of the Kingdom through the progressive use of human "means," albeit, to the greater glory of God. Human initiative and activity in this great new land would bring on the millennium and the Kingdom. Edwards represents the theologian *par excellence* of this new eschatological people called Americans when he writes:

> Thus Christ teaches us that it becomes his disciples to seek this above all other things, and make it the first and last in their prayers, and that every petition should be put up in a subordination to the advancement of God's kingdom and glory in the world.

ANOTHER ESCHATOLOGICAL PEOPLE

Not many of the African slaves, who were brought to the British colonies in North America, became Christians during the first one hundred and fifty years after their arrival in Jamestown, Virginia, in 1619. Perhaps fewer than 6 percent converted to Christianity. But those who became members of mission stations or joined the white churches were deeply impressed by the revival preaching of the Great Awakening of the 1730s and 1740s. The vision of New England Congregationalists such as Jonathan Edwards—that the millennium was coming and that Christians were called to prepare for it—reached them through the far-ranging missionary work of white evangelists such as Shubal Stearnes, Wait Palmer, and Matthew Moore—all of whom became Separatist Baptist preachers in the plantation country of Virginia, North and South Carolina, and Georgia.

The eschatological orientation of the slowly evolving independent black churches took a different twist from that of late Puritanism. It is not surprising that black Christians, who would remain in bondage for the next one hundred and thirty-three years, could not share the heady feeling that they were helping to build the Kingdom of God on earth that characterized the eschatology of white Americans. They were, in fact, puzzled by how they could be expected to participate in the great enterprise that seemed to excite everyone else when their white brothers and sisters in Christ insisted upon keeping them in chains. During the Revolutionary War period several groups of Christian slaves expressed that very concern in petitions to colonial legislatures.

The eschatology of the black church, therefore, took on a more "otherworldly" character. The hope that was commended to them in the preaching of the white missionaries was the hope of a life beyond the grave, beyond the misery and hardship of their daily existence—the hope of heaven. Black preachers, ordained and unordained, took up this same theme of deliverance from the woes of this world in their at first clandestine and then increasingly aboveground churches, under the surveillance if not the indirect supervision of white ministers. But there were other factors at work in the

development of black Christianity in the eighteenth and
nineteenth centuries that were to make the slaves another eschatological people on American soil who had a
somewhat different orientation from what they were
taught or heard expressed in the postmillennialism of
white Protestantism. Some of these factors were also
present on the continent of Europe in what has been
called the "left wing of the Reformation" and in seven-
teenth-century Puritanism. But one must not forget that
the black slaves in America were an *African* people—and
that makes it necessary to begin our discussion of their
eschatology from a different point of departure.

THE AFRICAN FACTOR

There continues to be a lively debate among scholars
about how much traditional African culture was retained
as the slaves in North America were subjected to Euro-
American culture. One side holds that, unlike the slaves
in the Caribbean and in Latin America, particularly those
under Roman Catholic custody, the slaves in the British
colonies of North America lost practically all of their
African inheritance under the peculiar conditions of their
enslavement and evangelization in Protestant North
America. The other side argues that while most of the
material culture of West Africa was lost among the
relatively few Africans sent to North America, enough of
the nonmaterial culture—i.e., the thought forms, music,
the dance, magic, and religion—was retained to have
some effect on their transition from an African to an
American identity. It is thought that this was particularly
true in the plantation areas of the South where blacks
were more heavily concentrated.

In recent years a more careful study of slavery from the
point of view of the slaves themselves and the investigation of neglected aspects of black culture in the United

States have tended to support the latter view. Today most scholars, white as well as black, would say that the African slaves did not arrive as clear slates upon which the colonists could write whatever they pleased, but that the ways of looking at themselves and the world in which they lived, their forms of recreation, religious practices, and other functions of life were combined in various ways with the culture of colonial America to produce a new and distinctive Afro-American culture. This Afro-Americanization, it is said, took place mainly between "sundown and sunup," in the slave cabins after the working day, and it represented something different from either a pure African or a pure Euro-American culture. What happened was the engrafting of the white society's ways upon an African base to produce not an American African but an Afro-American community.

Melville Herskovits, a white anthropologist, and W. E. B. Du Bois, a black sociologist, held independently the conviction that this could be seen most clearly in the institution of religion. Although the African gods did not survive more than a brief period on American soil, the indigenous African world view and traditional African spirituality did continue in the slave community. They were partly selective and partly unconscious factors in the new religion of black converts to Christianity up to and including the nineteenth century.

SOME IMPLICATIONS FOR ESCHATOLOGY

If black people became another eschatological people under the impact of Christianization in the New World, how did this happen? How did their eschatology differ from that of the Calvinistic churches of America? Here again we cannot go into great detail, but some basic considerations are necessary.

In his book *New Testament Eschatology in an African*

Background (1971), the African theologian John S. Mbiti
shows how traditional African concepts among his own
Akamba people of Kenya (but also among many tribes in
West Africa and elsewhere on the continent) related to
the eschatological preaching of European missionaries
and how the future hope in Christ was understood. Most
important was the difference between the three dimensions of time in the New Testament (past, present, and
future), as interpreted by the missionaries, and what are
essentially only two dimensions of time for African
people—the dynamic, intense "present" and the long,
myth-laden "past." The concept of an extended future,
many years hence and going on into infinity, is virtually
unknown to Africans, says Mbiti. Consequently, when
the white missionaries translated the New Testament
into the Akamba language and preached "Jesus will
come," they were understood to be saying (depending
upon the tense of the Akamba verb) either: (1) that he
would come in a few months, (2) immediately, now, (3) at
any time, but certainly before one's death, or (4) that he is
"just outside the house, right on the road coming and can
even be seen approaching the homestead." There were
no other possibilities in the language or the world view
of the African traditionalist.

Mbiti points out many of the misunderstandings and
distortions of the eschatological message of the gospel
that resulted from this encounter of two different ways of
looking at the world and at the Parousia. His study
provides some valuable hints for understanding why the
eschatology of the black American church turned out the
way it did—quite apart from all that we have heard about
otherworldliness and escapism. It helps us to understand
what happened when Afro-American slaves heard the
Edwardsian eschatology being preached to their masters,
or when the missionaries tried to translate it into the
pidgin English of the recently arrived Africans—being

careful to emphasize a future heaven over the possibility of freedom and social progress here on earth. Using Mbiti's analysis, even with due consideration for the differences between the situation of the Akamba in Kenya and the mixed tribal groups in tidewater Virginia or along the Savannah River, we can see why the "other-worldliness" of black religion in America is much more complex than we have assumed and contains glimpses of eschatological depths that go beyond the millennial perspectives of American revivalism. It is possible that they even go beyond what Mbiti would consider an appropriate expression of the Christian hope, given his own criticism of Christian eschatology as reinterpreted by African traditional religion.

The historic black churches of the eighteenth and nineteenth centuries succeeded in getting rid of most of their African heritage in the interest of becoming what they thought were "respectable ecclesiastical institutions" for a rising black middle class. As Du Bois noted, however, some traces of the African world view and spirituality continued to cling to their practices. We know, for example, that Daniel Alexander Payne, the distinguished bishop of the African Methodist Episcopal Church, had difficulty stamping out the "spiritual songs" and the African "ring shout" from A.M.E. worship services as late as the 1870s. The tenacity of the African practices was noted not only in isolated rural areas but in some of the better-known A.M.E. congregations in Baltimore and Washington.

It is in the beliefs and practices of the later black sects and cults, well into the twentieth century, that we can see most clearly how the African background that Mbiti investigates may have influenced eschatological ideas that continue to pervade black folk culture and make black Americans another eschatological people—with a difference

What we must do in the next chapter is uncover some of the responses of the slaves to millennial eschatology in the white church by tracing the early development of black religion in the United States. In such a way we may be able to see what are the differences between the eschatological hope embedded in black religion and culture and that hope as expressed in white Christianity, particularly in Protestant fundamentalism.

6

ESCHATOLOGY IN BLACK

It should be well known to Americans that the Christian slaves were an eschatological people who believed that Christ was coming again and that there would be a radical transformation of the world and in relationships between people. This is, unfortunately, not the case, because religious history in the United States has been written primarily by the dominant group. But when we look at the story of the faith from "the underside" another picture emerges.

In the Negro spiritual, the religious folk songs created by spontaneous combustion in the fields and cabins during the latter part of eighteenth and into the nineteenth century, there is much talk of the great impending event of the Final Coming:

> Yes one o' dese mornin's bout twelve o'clock,
> Dis ol' worl' am gwinter reel and rock.

> I want to be ready,
> I want to be ready,
> I want to be ready,
> To walk in Jerusalem just like John.

> Great day! Great day, the righteous marching.
> Great day! God's going to build up Zion's walls.

Literally hundreds of spirituals and other slave songs could be quoted to show without a doubt that the religion of the slaves contained strong eschatological elements reflecting various apocalyptic passages of the Bible, particularly from the book of Revelation. Take for example:

> Come down, come down, my Lord, come down,
> My Lord's a-writin' all de time;
> And take me up to wear the crown,
> My Lord's a-writin' all de time.
>
> O what a beautiful city,
> O what a beautiful city,
> O what a beautiful city,
> Twelve gates to the city, hallelu!

But what was the timetable of Jesus' appearance for the slaves, how did they deal with the delay, and what was the significance of their expectation for the development of black religion in America?

John S. Mbiti notes that the African converts in Kenya sang many similar songs and hymns that stressed the Final Coming even though, as he ruefully concedes, the absence of an appropriate verb tense to suggest the possibility of a long waiting period made for some misunderstanding and distortion of what he understands to be the authentic meaning of the biblical symbolism. We will return to that later, but now we must ask if it is possible to see some of these same "misunderstandings" and "distortions" working in Afro-American slave Christianity.

In view of what Mbiti has written concerning the traditional African concept of time (as pervasive in West Africa as in East), a conjecture can be made that the first slaves to hear the gospel preached in the New World must have had some of the same reactions as the Akamba people. The short future of the African world view—not more than five or six months hence—must have intensified the expectation of "Massa Jesus" whenever the missionary preaching included the millennial ideas that were articulated during the two Great Awakenings, one before and one after the Revolution. The poetry of the spirituals, with their strongest accent upon personal experience, makes it reasonable to believe that the intensity was even more exaggerated—stretched almost to a breaking point—by the brutality of the slave system. The backbreaking labor without wages, the constant fear of being sold "farther South" into even more intolerable conditions, were goads to millennial anticipations.

THREE BASIC RESPONSES OF THE SLAVES

There were, generally speaking, three basic responses to the preaching of the end of the world and the Parousia that can be illustrated by experiences of slave conversions reported by some of the missionaries, and found also in autobiographical slave narratives that were written or recorded. These responses roughly correlate with what sociologists call the passive and the aggressive, or accommodation and protest modes of behavior among an oppressed group. There are, however, two additional factors that have not always been considered in analyses of how black Americans responded to millennialist preaching: first, the absence of any concept of a long, indefinite future in the culture of African slaves, and secondly, the way the desire for gratification in the present, as a characteristic of that culture, was intensified by the unusual brutality of the institution of slavery in the Americas.

First, there was a turning away from Christianity altogether. Many slaves reacted to eschatological preaching in disbelief when it became obvious that nothing was going to happen within the time period that made sense to them. We know that millions never became church members and many backslid from their "conversions," much to the astonishment and dismay of the missionaries. In their reports of evangelization efforts many missionaries speak of apostasy on the plantations as a common occurrence. Some slaves were never convinced that the white preachers were telling the truth. Others believed and were baptized, but it seems that many, perhaps the majority, drew back from their original commitment and either returned to the remnants of their ancestral religions or believed nothing.

In any case, when the ministers and teachers of the Northern-based black denominations went South in the wake of the Union armies, they found thousands of former slaves who had heard about Christianity, but had not practiced it. These were soon to swell the ranks of the black churches. Those thousands who were drawn into the Methodist and Baptist churches following the war were undoubtedly attracted by hearing the gospel out of the mouth of someone of their own color. But we know that there was also a different message in that preaching from what they were accustomed to hearing from both the white Southern preachers and the white Northerners who frequently competed openly with the missionaries of the black denominations for new members among the recently freed people.

It is important to note also that even during this triumphant period of black Christianity many continued to stay outside the organized church (which is not to say that they did not have their own religion) and went into the twentieth century unchurched. Mbiti reports that some Akamba converts concluded that Christ may have "changed his mind" and will never come and that they should "eat and drink, for tomorrow we die." In the United States some former Christians certainly felt the same way. Some of them joined non-Christian or marginally Christian sects and cults in the urban ghettos of the North during the First World War and the Great Depression. This has been, of course, a common phenomenon in

Africa since the 1870s when thousands of independent or "Ethiopian" churches grew up beside the missions—evidence of disappointment and dissatisfaction with the imported religion of Europe and America. We know that many black sects and cults developed in the United States during the last decades of the nineteenth and the early twentieth century for the same reasons.

The second response of the American slaves which parallels the experience of African converts was the internalization of the excitement about the immediate return of Christ by the intensification of charismatic phenomena and spirit possession. Before the Civil War, Presbyterian minister Charles C. Jones, and other whites, reported that many converts were given to wild visions, dreams, "rousements," and other signs of altered states of consciousness. Spirit possession, having lost its identification with native African deities, was interpreted by black American Christians as the visitation of the Holy Spirit and often occurred at the time of baptism.

Baptism, as Mbiti comments, does not simply wash away sins, but "temporal limitations are neutralized, so that the soul arrives at its spiritual 'Promised Land,' and is enabled to derive sustenance from the powers of the Age to Come." Hebrews 6:4ff. expresses this idea, and slaves interpreted baptism against the African background of spirit possession experience. The eschatological hope of the gospel and the intense desire to be delivered from the painful reality of present woes were compressed into a single, dazzling moment of transcendence when the slave was transported to the Promised Land "across the Jordan, wide and cold," to the presence of the risen Savior. This Savior who did not come in fact therefore came in truth—in the overpowering experience of the Holy Spirit in communal worship. The emotional quality and so-called otherworldliness of slave religion was, at least partly, a way of squeezing into the dynamic present an expectation and excitement that could not be projected into a remote future given the traditional concept of time among many African people.

The way in which the new black urban working class related to Pentecostalism, with its strong premillennialist flavor in the late nineteenth and early twentieth centuries, supports this contention. The black Pentecostal experience was more of a dissociation experience— more of an alteration of identity and perception than its white counterpart. It was, in other words, an African more than a Euro-American experience. The black Pentecostal historian Leonard Lovett brings this out when he describes the great Azusa Street Revival of Los Angeles in 1906, when the whites withdrew (a year later) because of what they considered to be offensive "Africanisms" in the way black members received the baptism of the Holy Ghost.

What we are saying is that one of the typical responses of the slaves and their near descendants to eschatological preaching was the abandonment, at least momentarily, of the futurist idea of the coming of Christ and the adoption of an "immediatist" orientation. Christ came to the black Christian community in the ecstasy of worship, and many of the spirituals echo this idea in the refrain:

> I know my Lord has set me free,
> I'm in Him and He's in me!

The third response of the slaves to eschatological preaching is closely related to the second. It is, in fact, another aspect of the immediacy of authentic black spirituality in the interims between the experience of possession. Mbiti points out that the basic notion of "the next world" is a feature of all African societies. This does not contradict the absence of a remote future, but it does indicate that the future is sometimes pushed back into the present and the mythic past where it makes connec-

tion with the "living dead"—the belief that the ancestors
are still with us and are involved in every aspect of our
daily lives.

Mbiti writes, "The next world is the hereafter beyond
physical death . . . pictured exclusively in materialistic
terms which make that world more or less a carbon copy
of the present." Another way of putting it would be to say
that it is the present world turned upside down—a world
in which "the evil cease oppressing" and the "last shall
be first." But it is a world "not far from the physical
world" in that it is where the natural gestures, affections,
and relationships of this present world are validated and
fulfilled. Mbiti has some difficulty with this idea, but we
will deal with that later.

In both African and Afro-American religion the idea of
the next world, which is to say the Kingdom of God, is
not some highly mystical, spiritualized realm that floats
over the real world and has no connection with it. It is
peopled with the ancestors who are ever near, with
people we have known and loved, and it contains the
things of this world wonderfully transformed. In that
important sense it is the criterion of the present world, a
model of perfection which stands in judgment upon it.
What we have too glibly called the "otherworldiness" of
slave religion was the eschatological vision that made it
possible not only to experience that world ecstatically in
the present but to make it visible and tangible in materialistic terms in the daily realities of the believer's life.
Thus, as Miles Mark Fisher and other interpreters of the
slave bards tell us, "Steal Away to Jesus" often was used
as a signal on the Underground Railroad; "Crossing the
Jordan" and "Wade in the Water, Children" sometimes
meant getting across the Ohio River to free territory;
"Going to the Promised Land" not only meant heaven,
but the dawn of Emancipation Day on January 1, 1863.

The hope that is expressed in the spirituals and in

some of the later gospel songs of the contemporary black church is rooted in the desire for freedom and a better chance in this world—under the pressure of the "next one." The images called forth, therefore, are materialistic—expressing the deprivation of slavery but also a profound sense of the possibility of a different experience in this life when Christ is Lord, although his Lordship is frustrated by evil men.

Marc Connelly's parody of a black heaven in *The Green Pastures* is fatuously extravagant, but there are aspects of the play that do convey the worldliness and concreteness of the black religious imagination. Given the thin line between the sacred and the secular that is characteristic of African and Afro-American world views, it is not surprising that Father Divine, Daddy Grace, and other "black gods of the metropolis," with their heavens and retinues of flesh-and-blood angels, had mass appeal in the black urban communities during the 1920s and 1930s. The familiar spiritual "All God's Chillun" is a good example of the down-to-earth concreteness of black eschatology:

> I got a robe, you got a robe,
> All God's chillun got a robe,
> When I get to Heav'm, goin' put on my robe,
> Goin' to shout all over God's Heav'm,
> Heav'm, Heav'm,
> Everybody talking' 'bout Heav'm ain't goin' dere,
> Heav'm, Heav'm,
> Goin' to shout all over God's Heav'm!

The verse speaks of robes, shoes, crown, wings, harps, and songs. With the exception of crowns and wings, all of these images used by the slave poet refer to worldly things. They are not mystical accessories to the heavenly existence. To the contrary, they are understood to be basic to it—the fundamental earthbound rights and requirements of personal fulfillment, justice, freedom, and autonomy. With them in his or her possession the believer can "shout all over God's Heav'm" without the inhibition experienced in daily life. But what is represented here is not only what the believer has been denied on earth but the values by which the world is weighed in the balance and found wanting, by which it is called to account for not making life what God intended it to be in the first place—fulfilling, just, free, and autonomous.

During the civil rights movement the folk on the marches and at rallies sometimes added votes, schools, and seats (acceptance in places of public accommodation) to the traditional robes, shoes, and crowns. The notion of using votes "when I get to Heav'm" cannot be mistaken for an example of "compensatory religion" when those doing the singing are walking a voter registration picket line in open defiance of angry whites with guns. Something else is obviously at work here.

A DISTORTED ESCHATOLOGY?

In his discussion of the Akamba concept of "treasure in heaven," Mbiti is critical of how the traditional world view has "distorted" the symbolism of the gospel. He writes:

> It is relatively easy to transfer one's wishes for material benefits from the immediate environment of deprivation and want to a dreamland which in this case is identified with heaven. . . . Thus, the whole concept of heavenly treasure or riches is entirely divorced from Christ except insofar as He conveys people from the world of material deprivation to that of rewards and riches. What seems to be happening, therefore, is that the extension of the future is not possible in terms of Time *per se*, but only in a materialistic projection of people's experiences and wishes in this life. Even God is oriented toward the production or creation of that type of future—an intensely anthropocentric and physicalized future.

This is the main emphasis of his criticism of the "misunderstandings" and "distortions" of New Testament eschatology when filtered through African traditional religion. The Akamba, Mbiti believes, have taken the symbols of apocalyptic for the real thing, failing to grasp their theological meaning on the conceptual level. "Instead," he writes, "they have come out with a purely materialistic image of eschatological realities, which, in turn, create a false spirituality in their Christian living." But is this the only way to interpret what is going on?

It is at this point that we must question whether Mbiti appreciates the full significance of the reluctance of African people to draw a sharp difference between heaven and earth, the sacred and the profane, religion and life; this division is, of course, a well-known characteristic of the Western way of thinking. In any case, on this point we will argue that this characteristic of traditional African culture was a more positive influence for survival in America than Mbiti believes it was under colonialism in Kenya. It was precisely the desperateness of the Afro-American slaves, as contrasted with the African converts under European missionaries, that made what Mbiti calls a "false spirituality" in Kenya a more human and perhaps a more authentically Christian spirituality in the American South. The difference between the black experience in Africa and in the United States comes to light in his conclusions and must be noted here.

Several factors account for this difference: (1) the institution of chattel slavery forced the black slaves in America to fight one way or another for their humanity, or die; (2) the absence of a common language that could compete with the language of the white captors; (3) the absence of a single, vital tradition of non-Christian religion in the slave community; (4) being removed to a strange land and, in most instances in North America, being a numerical minority; (5) the subversive connections made between Christianity and emancipation by a few renegade white missionaries and preachers; (6) the rapid development of a quasi-independent leadership class in the slave community with strong secular as well as religious ambitions and motivations; and (7) the centrality of the church rather than the family or clan in Afro-American culture.

The Afro-American religious experience, *as a whole,* cannot be interpreted as regressive or "false spirituality." While there is certainly evidence of escapism and otherworldliness in black American religion, that is not the whole story. The general direction of black spirituality has been toward stubborn resistance by subterfuge and nonconformity in the interest of survival. It more frequently sought to transform existing reality by demanding a materialization of eschatological hope in a way that recalls the Hebraic background of New Testament eschatology.

SLAVE RELIGION AND THE BLACK CHURCH

We can conclude this discussion of the responses of slave religion to eschatological elements in the gospel (and, by extension, the responses of contemporary black Christianity) with the following observations:

1. The three major responses we have analyzed (however superficially) are not related exclusively to the carry-over of the African concept of time into black American culture. Other influences must be seen in America, including other elements of the African heritage, those coming from Native American religions (with which many slaves had close acquaintance), from white revivalism, and from the slaves' own perception of their situation and what needed to be done to deal with it.

2. Whatever may be true about Akamba Christianity, it is a mistake to regard black spirituality in America as

either crassly materialistic or hopelessly otherworldly.
The authentic faith of the black folk community brought
together this world and the next in a creative tension that
produced such sentiments as these expressed in the
spirituals:

> I'm so busy serving my Jesus,
> That I ain't got time to die.
>
> Marching up the heavenly road . . .
> I'm bound to fight until I die.
>
> Singin' wid a sword in ma han', Lord,
> Singing' wid a sword in ma han',
> In ma han', Lord,
> Singin' wid a sword in my han'.
>
> O Freedom, O Freedom, O Freedom over
>   me,
> And before I'd be a slave,
> I'd be buried in my grave,
> And go home to my Lord and be free!

It was the acquaintance of Afro-American people with
"a fight for life," with the experience of suffering and
struggle that gave them an eschatology that took the
message of liberation in the Old and New Testaments
and welded them to the base of an African spirituality,
and to fading but still vital elements of the African world
view. The result was a new eschatological perspective
for Christianity in America. It arose in the sanctuary as
the ecstasy of a vision of paradise at one moment, and in
the next it drove believers into the streets to give that
vision material actuality in the structures of society. In
the worship experience of the black congregation Jesus
Christ came every Sunday as the guarantor of a new
reality "for all God's children"—bringing to naught the
things that are and bringing into existence the things that
do not yet exist (I Cor. 1:28).

3. Finally, it is no accident that Dr. Martin Luther
King, Jr., chose the "I Have a Dream" speech at the

Lincoln Memorial in Washington, D.C., on August 28, 1963, to articulate the profoundly eschatological meaning of the black struggle for "jobs and freedom." Nor is it surprising that he died in Memphis, where he had set up his headquarters in Mason Temple, the "cathedral church" of the Church of God in Christ, the largest of the so-called "otherworldly" black Pentecostal denominations. He was in Memphis to support a garbage workers strike of a union made up primarily of members of the Church of God in Christ.

King was, after all, a black Baptist preacher who had grown up in the culture and religious tradition of the black folk. Although he had varnished it with the erudition and sophistication of a Boston University Ph.D., he knew the power of the vision that excited and motivated black people and that lay at the heart of traditional black religion. It was an eschatological vision of the Kingdom of God as liberation from sin, slavery, and second-class citizenship, but also as freedom from bigotry, hatred, and the alienation of people from one another in the land of their birth and common destiny. And so he preached that hot August afternoon just as he preached at the Dexter Avenue Baptist Church in Montgomery, or in his father's pulpit at Ebenezer Baptist Church in Atlanta:

I say to you today, my friends, that, even though we face the difficulties of today and tomorrow, I still have a dream. It is a dream deeply rooted in the American dream. . . . I have a dream that one day on the red hills of Georgia sons of former slaves and sons of former slave-owners will be able to sit down together at the table of brotherhood. I have a dream that one day even the state of Mississippi, a desert state sweltering with the heat of injustice, sweltering with the heat of oppression, will be transformed into an oasis of freedom and justice. . . . I have a dream that one day every valley shall be exalted, every hill and mountain shall be made low, the rough places will be made plain, and the crooked places will be made straight, and the glory of the

Lord shall be revealed, and all flesh shall see it together.
This is our hope. This is the faith that I go back to the South
with. With this faith we will be able to hew out of the
mountain of despair a stone of hope.

For King and for many others who heard him that day,
it was not a dream of something impossible of realization—a mere oratorical flourish that black preachers
sometimes use as much to entertain as to edify. It was not
a dream for some distant future beyond history when
Jesus would descend with a clap of thunder and a blast of
heavenly trumpets. It was a dream of the Kingdom of
God in which marching people, black and white, Jew
and Gentile, lined up to be registered to vote, challenged
segregated schools and lunch counters, overturned the
tables of economic exploitation and job discrimination. It
was, in short, a dream to be brought into reality by the
struggles and sacrifices of the people of God. King would
not have used such an eschatological symbol at this
crucial event if he had not known of its wide acceptance
in the black community—and especially in the black
church.

Whether or not this dream has been or could be
actualized is another question that does not really concern us at the moment. What is important is that in this
famous address at the March on Washington, King represented the historic tradition of black Christianity at its
best—the faith of another eschatological people who had
come to these shores in chains, but who had not given up
hope, a people for whom the promises of "a new heaven
and a new earth" were to be taken as both spiritual and
material possibilities in the present. For this tradition to
say that "Jesus Christ is coming" was to make an eschatological statement that was both religious and secular, and
it was within the competence of believers to experience
both the spirit and the substance of this eschatology in
the world in which they lived.

THE WHITE CHRISTIAN EXPERIENCE

It is time for us to ask: Is this perspective absent from white Christianity? That question is often asked of those who have made a study of black religion and seem to be making exclusive claims for it. The answer is both yes and no.

Obviously it is not possible to separate the development of black and white religious beliefs and practices in the United States. An indigenous American Christianity grew up and flourished on the frontier and on the plantations of the South. Blacks and whites participated in it together and learned from one another at the revivals and camp meetings that are so much a part of American religious history. The majority of black Christians of the South between 1830 and 1861—the period of the greatest effort to convert the slaves—either worshiped with white people (albeit, in segregated pews) or were under the supervision of white pastors and missionaries. In those situations it is likely that the white worshipers were more impressed by the black worshipers than vice versa, because of the powerful impact of black singing, praying, testifying, and other aspects of their devotional style coming out of the African background and the rigors of slavery. But what was not taught to them by the whites was "caught," and the early history of the old Colored Methodist Episcopal Church (now Christian Methodist Episcopal Church)—the first black denomination founded in the South—illustrates how white tutelage affected the development of black Christianity. Other examples could be cited, but there is little argument against the importance of the role of white churches in the institutionalization of black Christianity.

The eschatology of the mainstream of the Protestant denominations developed in a strong postmillennialist direction under the impulse of what has been called

"ethical revivalism" and the missionary movements of
the nineteenth century. The Social Gospel movement
was one of the consequences of that development.

There are, therefore, eschatological elements in the
belief and practices of white Christians in the United
States that parallel those in the segregated black
churches. Both faiths have strong empirical tendencies
encased in an underlying supernaturalism or "otherworldliness." Both churches have contributed to the
amazing versatility and social activism of American
Christianity, and the close connection between social
action and the kind of evangelism that goes out "to save
the world in this generation"—before Jesus comes.

On the other hand, the black churches have never
been torn apart by the fundamentalist-modernist controversy about the Bible and theology that divided white
Protestantism in the first half of this century and continues to plague it. Secondly, black Christians have generally been at the bottom of the socioeconomic ladder. They
have been the outs rather than the ins. They have,
therefore, been less disposed than white middle-class
Christians to sanctify the American Way of Life and use
religion for integrative and consensus purposes rather
than for protest and class struggle. Thirdly, white Christianity in the United States developed out of a Western
rationalistic concept of reality and world view, while
black Christianity—with allowances for adaptations it
has made—developed out of an African, spiritual concept
of life.

These two modes of looking at the world and position-
ing the self in relation to its future have come together at
several points and are now battling with each other on
the continent of Africa and in the Third World generally.
But cultures do not change as rapidly as they seem to on
the surface. The difference between these two perspectives has produced a biblical literalism and an intellectu-

al, polemical form of fundamentalism in the white church that is barely known in the black church, except marginally in a relatively late movement—and even there, tenuously, as we saw in Chapter 4.

Black Christianity in America has deficiencies. It has suffered from ethnic parochialism, anti-intellectualism, and unrepentant disunity since its inception, and it is not clear that the rising middle-class status of its members will cure these most serious maladies. Many of the classic problems of mainstream white denominations are now showing up in black denominations. But it is also true that black churches, in the main, have been able to retain some of the lineaments of their African or non-Western inheritance as blacks continue to preserve an ethnic-specific culture. The faith of the black folk may be eroding today, but at the beginning of the 1980s—largely as a result of the black consciousness of the last twenty years—it continues to have vitality. Black faith has so far been successful in avoiding some of the more troubling aspects of white Christianity in the United States.

Vine Deloria, Jr., the Native American attorney and theologian, may exaggerate the principal characteristics of white Christianity in his provocative book *God Is Red* (1973), but what he has to say about it points out the differences between black and white spirituality:

> Contemporary American Christianity can quite possibly be understood as having two major, apparently mutually exclusive, emphases. The right-wing, evangelical, and fundamentalist spectrum of Christianity dwells almost exclusively and fanatically on the figure of Jesus, and on the theology of the old-time religion. . . . The predominance of white men in the right-wing of Christianity and their perpetual identification of Christianity as the opponent and mortal enemy of Communism, Socialism, freethinking, long hair, and other symbolic foes makes their version of Christianity little more than a sacred patriotism seeking to restore the imagined elegance of the last century to Ameri-

can society. Their position with respect to social problems
is generally to ignore them. . . . The left-wing is almost the
opposite of its counterpart. It is probably best represented
by the more traditional denominations such as the Presby-
terians, Methodists, United Church of Christ, Episcopa-
lians, and Roman Catholics. . . . They feel the only task
remaining in the field of religion is to find a way to make
their church relevant to the outside world. Most of them
would take the Second Coming of Jesus as a personal
affront indicating that God has lost confidence in their
ability to solve problems.

Too simplistic? Deloria's profiles may be too sharply
drawn. But this long quotation expresses well the main
argument of black theologians like James H. Cone and J.
Deotis Roberts, who have attempted, in different ways,
to help the black denominations escape this split in
white theology—to "hold on to Jesus" while passing the
ammunition for an all-out assault on the status quo. They
agree with Deloria that white conservative Christians are
generally in favor of the military-industrial complex of
power in the United States. They would contend that
conservative theology and reactionary politics come together in a common opposition to systemic change for a
more equitable distribution of wealth, greater justice for
minorities and women, and greater American support for
social revolutions in the Third World—for example, the
struggle for majority rule in South Africa. These are
action programs they recommend to the black church. In
the view of Cone and others, they are the moral implications of Dr. King's "beloved community" and the natural
outgrowth of the eschatological hope he talked about.

Despite all we have said about the "pragmatic spirituality" of black faith, it is a mistake to expect it to produce
the same kind of crusading social activism that Deloria
parodies in his description of the left wing of white
Christianity. Christians who take the Kingdom of God
seriously cannot withdraw from the world without sur-

rendering it to the structures of evil. The black church has shared this concern for responsible Christian participation in the world with progressive elements in the white community, and has had more urgent reasons for doing so.

Yet black Christianity, in its traditional form, shares with premillennialism the belief that the *visible* reign of Christ does not come by social action programs, but rather by catastrophe. It is of the nature of Afro-American spirituality to be suspicious of projects to "erect the Kingdom of God on earth," even while it provides the motive power for Christian political action—one of its strongest suits. As one black theologian of the 1960s, Nathan Wright, Jr., has pointed out, the object of black religion is not doing good or making the world better, but the experience of the glory of God. Rationalistic, programmatic social action seldom finds enthusiastic support in the black denominations, not because the people and their leaders are politically reactionary or willing to wait for a supernatural transformation of the world, but because black faith is humble and unpretentious about human capabilities.

There is a tragic motif in black faith that comes out of the experience of suffering. Black faith knows a great deal about the cross. That is why James H. Cone is correct in his contention that "Black theology rejects as invalid the oppressors' attempt to escape the question of death." He is careful to walk the fine line in black eschatology between resignation as a negative response to the promises of spiritual salvation and the delusion of omnipotence that make some Christians believe that they can have heaven on earth. He writes:

> Heaven cannot mean accepting injustice of the present because we know we have a home over yonder. Home is where we have been placed now, and to believe in heaven is to refuse to accept hell on earth. . . . But there is another

dimension that we must protect despite white corruption of it. Black theology cannot reject the future reality of life after death—grounded in Christ's resurrection—simply because white people have distorted it for their own selfish purposes.

It is difficult to articulate this central paradox of black eschatology, and Cone does not altogether succeed in his discussion in *A Black Theology of Liberation* (1970). Perhaps it can only be expressed in the poetry of the spirituals. It is no accident that John Lovell, Jr., in his almost exhaustive analysis of the spirituals, *Black Songs: The Forge and the Flame* (1972), places side by side the songs that deal with the determination "to struggle, resist and hold fast" with those about heaven. He observes that the spirituals frequently use the "soldier theme"—the call to fight for black manhood and womanhood in a hostile world:

> O stay in the field, children-ah
> Stay in the field, children-ah,
> Stay in the field,
> Until the war is ended.
> I've got my breastplate, sword and shield,
> And I'll go marching thro' the field,
> Till the war is ended.

But there is also the emphasis that the time will come when "I'm going to lay down my sword and shield, down by the riverside, to study war no more." The true eschatological hope of black faith is sounded in that spiritual, and triumphantly in one that is heard more frequently in black churches today:

> I've a crown up in the Kingdom,
> Ain't that good news!
> I've a crown up in the Kingdom,
> Ain't that good news!
> Goin' to lay down this world,
> Goin' to shoulder up my cross,
> Goin' to take it home to Jesus,
> Ain't that good news!

7

FOLLOWING THE LEADER
IN LIFE AND DEATH

At the beginning of this book we talked about children and the childlike innocence that Jesus identified with the Kingdom of God. Now we return to that theme in this concluding chapter about following the Leader—by which we mean *discipleship*—into the daily demands of our life together and the shadow of what must necessarily be our separate deaths. This is, after everything has been said, where any discussion of Christian eschatology must end.

Many of us as children played the game Follow the Leader. I particularly remember playing it in (of all places!) a huge abandoned cemetery that used to be at 25th and Diamond Streets in North Philadelphia where I was born. That cemetery was like a playground for our neighborhood, the only playground we had in those days. After most of the remains had been removed to another cemetery the city built its first low-income housing project over the empty graves.

As everyone knows, in Follow the Leader one has to do everything the leader does or must fall out of the game. If, in our case, the leader turned over a garbage can as he ran through an alley, everyone who followed had to turn over a garbage can. If the leader leaped over an open pit where a large family was once interred, or climbed up the face of a crumbling statue, or threw an old bone out of a grave he had jumped into, everyone else had to do the same—no shortcuts! The leader was, as I recall, usually the strongest and most daring boy in the crowd. Many were the times that I ran after whoever was our leader that day, shouting, laughing, doing my best to keep up and imitate his antics!

Analogies are notoriously inexact, but Jesus is our strong and daring leader who, nevertheless, exhibited the weakness of our mortality. To be a Christian means to follow this Leader. No one should be confused about that one simple fact which theologians have sometimes made more difficult than it should be. Only those who at least *try* to follow Christ have the right to use his name to name themselves—to call themselves *Christ-ians*. Just as we boys ran behind our plucky leader, sniffing at what he sniffed at, spitting at what he spat at, rolling over where he rolled over, and disappearing into caves into which he disappeared—and just as the loyalty and solidarity of our crowd was expressed by that kind of cohesion-building or bonding activity—so do Christians follow Jesus and are bound together by commitment and loyalty as they follow him all the way.

I remember that there were many mounds and caves in that old abandoned cemetery. That is one of the things that suggests the analogy to me—in this sense: *one day Jesus disappeared into a dark cave at the bottom of life,* a cave called death. He entered it willingly and bravely, despising the finality and shame of it. And we who trust him must follow him with the same attitude he had.

On that day when you and I take our last breath we will be challenged to take it as he took his and, with that same equanimity, to follow him into that unknown cavern from which none of us will ever return in this flesh.

"Oh," someone will say, "you are making it all sound

so glum! That's not so bad after all, is it? There was, you know, the resurrection."

Yes, the fact that eyewitnesses have left us the testimony that something happened to Jesus on the other side of that cave gives us hope. We have been talking about that throughout this book. But even if the eyewitness accounts are found to be perplexingly different, even if we cannot be sure about what really happened that morning, even if it were not part of the story, the real test of Christianity would have to be our faith, and that faith as *Christian* would stand or fall on whether or not we have the loyalty, obedience, and the guts to follow our Leader with the courage he had, with his prayer in Luke's witness—"Father, into thy hands I commit my spirit!"— and with the quiet, trusting faith he had when he bowed his head and entered into that yawning hole in the great cemetery of life.

That is what Christianity is all about—playing Follow the Leader with Jesus in everything we do, every day of our lives, all the way to the moment of our death and beyond. Those are the rules of the game. If we do not want to play it that way, we ought to fall out and do something else to occupy our time on this side of the cave of death. We will slip through it anyway. We only have to make up our minds *how*.

FOLLOWING IN DAILY WORK

We do not follow Jesus alone but with the church. The church is the community of those who follow the Leader in life and work. It preserves and passes on the eschatological message of salvation through his reconciling death and traces his footpath through the highways and hedges of life. The church seeks the will of its Leader by prayer, by the study of Scripture, and by looking for evidences of his presence in the world and joining him where he is at work.

Wherever there is hunger, thirst, estrangement, nakedness, ill health, and imprisonment the church looks for Jesus and ministers in his name, remembering that he said, "As you did it to one of the least of these my brothers and sisters, you did it to me" (Matt. 25:40). The church has no mission of its own. It is Christ's mission in the world, seeking those who are lost and unconcealing the presence of his Kingdom that is just beyond the horizon toward which the church marches, while the light of the Kingdom streams forth from the future to illumine the dark places of the present.

In life we walk through the shadow of death. What is it that keeps us going in the face of that somber reality? For some of us the knowledge that death is ever working in our bodies to "do us in" and that over all of our striving hangs the sentence of death is too much to contemplate with serenity and continue to take work seriously. It is so much the worse for good people who suffer beyond any just desert or reasonable explanation. Job's wife, sensing his bewilderment, told him to "curse God and die." Arthur Schopenhauer wrote that ours was the worst of all possible worlds and that to give oneself to work for a better one was nothing more than a refined egoism. The only worthy virtue for him was pity. Both H. L. Mencken and Clarence Darrow believed that death is the bitter end of a meaningless life.

The Christian does not find in the concept of immortality his or her reason for rejecting this pessimism, and continuing to live and work under the shadow of death, but in following Jesus with the childlike faith he himself expressed when healing the man born blind: "We must work the works of him who sent me, while it is day; night comes, when no one can work" (John 9:4). It is enough that the Leader is involved in the work of his Kingdom in

the world—bringing love, justice, truth, and freedom—
and that he calls us to follow him by doing that same
work as long as daylight lasts. We do not always even
understand the reason for the work or know its consequences. Jesus said that the man was not born blind
because of his or his parents' sins, but that the works of
God might be revealed, that God might be glorified. The
glory of God is the sign and completion of his Kingdom
and we have been called to do the work of that Kingdom
in our daily occupations, quite apart from either known
causes or guaranteed consequences.

When our work contributes to God's ongoing creation
and preservation of the world, when by a word or a deed
we help someone along the way, when by our labor some
space opens up for freedom or some injustice is challenged—whether or not we accomplish everything we
think we should—it is the work of him who sends us and
that is the only justification it needs. Whatever it may be,
when we do our daily work faithfully it is working
behind, and yet at the same time, in the company of our
Leader. It is, therefore, precisely what is required of
disciples that they be found faithful, nothing more and
nothing less. This is eschatology for daily life and work.
As Dr. Martin Luther King, Jr., said, "The end of life is
not to be happy nor to achieve pleasure and avoid pain,
but to do the will of God, come what may."

Anyone who follows Jesus in his or her daily work,
whatever the occupation or vocation, will find it linked to
God's purposes for the world and therefore in opposition
to the powers of evil personified by Satan or the devil.
Such work will always be carried on in the shadow of
death, in struggle and sacrifice, and with no guarantee of
success. But the eschatological meaning of work, behind
and in the company of Jesus, is that it is *his* work that we
perform, and since in this work he precedes us he also
waits for us at the end.

The young poet H. von Heintschel-Heinegg, one of the leaders of the Austrian resistance during the Second World War, wrote in his farewell letter before going to Hitler's guillotine in December 1944:

> The higher we climb, and the harder we fight, the more we participate in the work and struggle of Jesus Christ, whom the devil sought to confront in all manner of forms . . . and suffering thus with him (which means of course also fighting) and struggling with him, we become victors with him. Second, the higher we climb, and the harder we fight, the more grace, light, illumination, and strength and promise do we draw down upon ourselves—yes, draw down forcibly, especially the grace of the Cross and the grace of Pentecost, in other words, grace born of the suffering of redemption and of the struggle of fulfillment.

FOLLOWING IN SICKNESS AND DEATH

Eschatology has special meaning for those who are following the Leader in illness or at the twilight of life. If statistics are correct, many people who read this book will probably die of cancer or of an ailment of the circulatory system—lingering, perhaps, on this side of the cave longer than makes sense to them because they have been left so little use for their bodies. How does one follow Jesus at this critical juncture of life, at the very end of the game, in terminal illness and death?

The church is not only the community of followers in life and work; it is also the community of those who follow the Leader in death. Death is not an unwarranted and implausible part of what we are about in life. It is of its essence. We are dying every day, and a part of the affirmation of life and making it more abundant by daily service to the world is learning how to die with courage and confidence in God. Learning how to die as the Leader died is an important part of following him.

Each member of the church is an individual person

and each has to do his or her stunts alone even though
the church is a corporate entity, the one body of Christ.
But the fact that we all must follow the Leader through
that same dark cave at the bottom of life makes it good for
us continually to encourage one another, to depend on
one another for strength as long as we can, to reach out
and touch the next person as we approach, one at a time
but somehow together, the moment of our death. Somehow there is a feeling of continuity and structure in
knowing that we are all bound by the same rules—
something comforting and reassuring about knowing that
others are in front of and behind us—that we are all going
in the same direction together.

Donald C. Wilson, whose book *Terminal Candor*
(1978) describes how Christian faith sustained him in his
losing fight with cancer, writes about "walking through
the valley of the shadow of death":

> When the fact of our dying first comes home to us, our
> reaction is often to take to our heels and either run pell-
> mell for the light at the end of the tunnel or try to slither
> past the harsh realities by ignoring them. Not so with the
> Psalmist. He is willing to "walk" through them, taste them,
> if you will, as another aspect of the mystery of life ...
> moving through it at that pace we have time to get used to
> the darkness. In that darkness we may be able to detect
> what we have not noticed before—that there are others
> with us in the same shadow. They too are lonely, grieved,
> frightened and as much in the need of our hands as we are
> in need of theirs ... hand can reach out and touch hand,
> fears can be shared, burdens can be lifted. Like the
> Psalmist we may find that, never more so than in the valley
> of dying, we are in the presence of God.

The meaning and purpose of being a Christian, therefore, cannot be found in some kind of solitariness, some
private relationship to Jesus Christ. When we are at the
inevitable point of life called death, we realize how
important it is to be a member of this eschatological

community called the church—the community of those
who must follow the Leader right through the cave called
death.

Christian eschatology takes on a dynamic, communal
meaning about our nature and destiny as human beings
who have been invited to follow Jesus across this final
obstacle. It is not simply "the doctrine of the last things"
in the sense of being a description of the catastrophic end
of the world and the geography of heaven and hell. It is
an understanding, an unshakable conviction for this
present life—a belief in and joyous celebration of Jesus'
words: "My sheep hear my voice, and I know them, and
they follow me; and I give them eternal life, and they
shall never perish, and no one shall snatch them out of
my hand" (John 10:27–28). Eschatology is the church's
faith and confidence in the promises of Scripture by
which we follow Jesus through the challenges and demands of daily discipleship, experiencing now the eternal life he has already given, and looking forward with
the hope "that neither death, nor life, nor angels, nor
principalities, nor things present, nor things to come . . .
will be able to separate us from the love of God in Christ
Jesus our Lord" (Rom. 8:38–39).

The Christian hope of heaven rests ultimately upon
the promise of a God who is faithful and can be depend-
ed upon to keep a promise. It is not something of which
we need to be embarrassed. When we are suffering the
hell of this life, wracked with the pain of deteriorating
flesh in the terminal stages of a fatal disease, who would
deny the followers of Christ this hope so clearly promised in Scripture? And yet the agony of the Leader who
endured the cross and cried out, "My God, my God, why
hast thou forsaken me?" (Mark 15:34) must disabuse us
of any notion that when we follow him, there is a way out
easier than the one he suffered. Heaven, as Donald C.
Wilson wisely reminds us, must sometimes be held in

abeyance until the last measure of faithfulness has been wrung from us as it was from Jesus. Wilson writes:

> We tell ourselves that the remainder of our life with its anticipated troubles, including death itself, is of little count compared with the joys of heaven. So, rather than using faith's resources to give meaning to life's heartaches, we use them to pole-vault into a premature refuge in the life after death. The Apostle Paul found himself tempted by this very option of going "to be with Christ." But on reflection he decided that rather than putting all his eggs in the heavenly basket, God still had work for him here.

On the other hand, an eschatology that cannot conceive of a heaven cannot have taken the resurrection seriously. The hope of heaven is not some antiquated delusion about a fairyland in the sky which has long since been rendered untenable by the collapse of the three-tiered universe under the impact of the scientific study of astronomy. To hope in heaven is to believe that what awaits us after death is not nothing but *something,* something more closely related to God than anything known in this life—an existence in the eternal presence of God. To say that it is nothingness would be to hope, in our sinfulness, to escape from God in some way, and that is "unhopeable." Says the Psalmist:

> Whither shall I go from thy Spirit?
> Or whither shall I flee from thy presence?
> If I ascend to heaven, thou art there!
> If I make my bed in Sheol, thou art there!
> (Ps. 139:7–8)

So whatever lies on the other side of the cave cannot be total darkness, nothing—or something that places us beyond the power and presence of God. We have a much more positive anticipation, however difficult it may be to maintain it in the face of modern science. Our Leader said that he was returning to the Father and called us to follow him without anxiety or fear. He said that a "room"

or "home" would be prepared for us that we might be
where he is. That home can only mean some kind of
existence in the presence of God where our weary souls
can be at rest as we wait for the ultimate consummation
of God's purpose for the whole creation.

We may wish for more, but we have nothing to rely on
except the Leader's promise, his invitation, and his
resurrection. Our faith is that he is indeed the Life and
the Way he said he was. Our hope is that if we follow him
all the way we will share in that *something,* that it will be
unimaginably beautiful, and that all this will be made
manifest to us "at the proper time by the blessed and
only Sovereign, the King of kings and Lord of lords, who
alone has immortality and dwells in unapproachable
light, whom no person has ever seen or can see" (I Tim.
6:15–16). More than this we cannot say. We only follow
in silent hope.

FOLLOWING IN STRUGGLE AND CELEBRATION

In this chapter our primary focus has been upon the
church, for the message of hope in the resurrection
cannot be found or affirmed except in the church of
Christ. It is in this eschatological community and among
this people called Christians that the Holy Spirit bears
witness with our spirits that there is more to life than
what we experience between birth and death. The
church's theology will doubtlessly continue to change.
In the future greater emphasis will be placed on the
responsibility of Christians to transform this present
world where lust for power, greed, and selfishness have
so greatly contributed to a bitter life for most of the
people of the world. But if and when the hope of heaven
is given up by the church, it will no longer be the church
of Jesus Christ. The true church will always teach that, if

we follow Jesus in faith and obedience, death has no terror and life no end. We go to meet our Leader and we will find in him a victory that is not available on this side of the grave.

That good news is not only a source of comfort and encouragement for the "weary traveller." It is the reason for joy and celebration every time Christians come together for worship. The church is a "eucharistic *followership*"; its worship is a sacrament of thanksgiving and joy for the victory we now have and will experience in its totality when we join the Leader on the other side. It is this victory which we celebrate every Sunday, as the writer of Colossians puts it, as you "sing psalms and hymns and spiritual songs with thankfulness in your hearts to God" (Col. 3:16).

It is not difficult to be joyous and thankful when things are going well; when you live on the right side of town, have a good job and money in the bank. A church has no great problem with celebration when it is comfortable, affluent, and enjoying prestige and power in the world. But when your humanity is threatened every day, when you live in a rat-infested slum and have no job to go to in the morning, when the neighborhood schools are a disgrace and your church is in a decrepit building long since abandoned by others, or a ramshackle storefront whose address even the mail carrier is doubtful about— then celebration of the Christian life and death is a true measure of faith and hope. Since slavery the repudiation of the terror of dying, the celebration of life with all its hardness and struggle, and the hope of heaven have been at the root of the black Christian experience. All that the church has meant to the progressive development and liberation of the community, notwithstanding, without these characteristics of the people's faith it would have disappeared long ago.

Olin P. Moyd deals with this essential aspect of the
faith of a pilgrim people (*Redemption in Black Theology,*
1979):

> Final mending of the fission which exists between God
> and humankind is the ultimate end of Christian strivings.
> The Christian hope is that human beings will be eventual-
> ly brought back to a relationship with the Eternal which is
> consistent with his will in creation. The idea of heaven,
> then, the term masses of Black folks used instead of the
> term "eschatology," is essential to Black theology.

Attending a black worship service several years ago
one would likely have heard the spiritual "Nobody
knows the trouble I've seen, Glory Hallelujah!" It is a
slave song that fuses together, in one outpouring of
religious feeling, a complaint of trouble in this world and
a joyful acclamation of glory in the next; a cry of despair
and a shout of victory. Today the modern gospel songs
have largely replaced such spirituals in the typical black
worship service and something of the power and authen-
ticity of the faith of an oppressed people has been lost.
But in many churches the spiritual is coming back and
the more recent gospel music has retained much of the
affirmation of life and the eschatological hope of the
earlier generation.

The Harlem pastor and church musician Wyatt Tee
Walker believes that contemporary gospel, which has
much to say about "Going Up Yonder," "Heaven's My
Home," and "He'll Be Waiting at the End for Me," does
not diminish the connection between struggle for liberation and eschatological anticipation in the music of the
black church. Walker traces the development from the
spirituals of slavery, to *historic* gospel music during the
Great Depression, to *modern* gospel music which accom-
panied the radical struggle and social change of the King
era. "The creation of Gospel music," he writes, "is a social statement that, in the face of America's rejection and

economic privation, Black folks made a conscious decision to be themselves. . . . It suggested a return to 'roots' "
(*Somebody's Calling My Name: Black Sacred Music
and Social Change*, 1979). Those roots are a form of Christianity in which spirited preaching and joyously resound-
ing singing blend together words, melody, percussive
rhythm, and performatory style. The result is a seemingly
uninhibited but actually a socially regulated expression
of toughness and the determination to "overcome some-
day." Underneath the stylistic surface of black ritual on
Sunday morning is a poignant yearning for another
world—a transcendent experience of grace and glory.
The concern for secular liberation has become crucial in
black theology and increasingly in the contemporary
black church, but it has not replaced the faith expressed
by the great gospel composer Thomas A. Dorsey.

> When I've worked the last service,
> When I've helped the last soul,
> When I've left care behind me,
> When His face I behold—
> Well, I will tell Him my troubles
> And the load I had to bear.
> When I've sung my last song here,
> You'll find me singing over there.

We have said before in this book that black Christians
have no monopoly on an authentic faith for Americans. It
is true, nevertheless, that their distinctive approach to
eschatology has something to commend it to a church
that seeks to participate in the struggle for a new world
order and yet hold on to its vision of the Kingdom of God
in heaven. Since the 1960s the discussion about eschatology has fluctuated between utopian social activism and a
premillennial otherworldliness that has too easily avoid-
ed the realities of world oppression and the struggle of
millions at home and abroad to overcome it. In the
meantime, as the divided church loses its grip on the

historic faith, men and women struggle for justice without either the satisfaction of a politically supportive church or the sense of the forgiveness of their sins by the death and resurrection of Christ; they die without either the temporal vindication of their striving in the name of Christ or the hope of heaven. We have made the gospel ineffectual on both scores.

If the German theologian Wolfhart Pannenberg correctly states our current understanding of the eschatological consciousness as one that realizes "a power determining the present without thereby losing its futurity" (*Basic Questions in Theology,* 1970), then the affirmation of the meaning of struggle and suffering in this life, inseparable from the affirmation of life to come, should be welcomed by all Christians as a continuing contribution to eschatology. Those affirmations have been the keystone of the faith edifice of the black church in America, and it has been too long dismissed by white theologians as either the basis for a "civil rights religion" or for "pie in the sky when you die." It is neither—not a crassly materialistic this-worldliness nor a hopelessly irrelevant otherworldliness. From Richard Allen, the founder of the African Methodist Episcopal Church in the late eighteenth century, to Martin Luther King, Jr., the preacher of nonviolence and liberation in the twentieth, the black church has preserved the unity of struggle and "waiting upon the Lord," of secularity and eschatological hope, of the kingdoms of this world and the Kingdom of God.

In 1936, W. E. B. Du Bois delivered an address on the contributions of blacks to the nation and the state at the Hall of Negro Life of the Texas Centennial Exposition. He reiterated one of the powerful and recurring themes of his life's work—the need for America to take cognizance and advantage of "the peculiar spiritual quality" of black life and culture, and the significance of the church as a conservator of this quality which was so rapidly evaporating from the unhallowed, capitalistic ethos of the United States. Dr. Du Bois spoke of the religious genius of "the Negro priest" and the sensitivity to spiritual values of the black church. We would do well to heed his words today:

> This, then, is the gift of black folk to the New World. Thus in singular and fine sense the slave became master, the bond servant became free, and the meek not only inherited the earth, but made the heritage a thing of questing for eternal youth, of fruitful labor, of joy and music, of the free spirit and of the ministering hand, of wide and poignant sympathy with men in their struggle to live and love, which is, after all, the end of being

This image of the Kingdom of love and liberty, of the soul-gift of black folk, is a good expression of an eschatological consciousness for all who would follow Jesus Christ into the future. It provides the best reason for us to overcome the estrangement between black and white churches in this country—to accept and give thanks for the gifts we bring to each other "out of the gloomy past," and to begin a search for opportunities and means to follow the one Lord together. In this way we can break through the separatedness which scandalizes Christianity before this nation and join a partnership in this mission to an understandably skeptical and unbelieving world. Only so will the church in America be ready for him for whom our hearts yearn—the Leader who was, and is, and will be in the future—and be able to sing Charles Wesley's great hymn with conviction.

> Come, Thou long-expected Jesus,
>   Born to set Thy people free;
> From our fears and sins release us:
>   Let us find our rest in Thee.
> Israel's Strength and Consolation,
>   Hope of all the earth Thou art:
> Dear Desire of every nation,
>   Joy of every longing heart.

QUESTIONS FOR DISCUSSION

Chapter 1. LIFE, THE BIBLE, AND JESUS CHRIST

1. What is actually going on in the three illustrations on p. 14? How are facts often used to destroy the very truth they are supposed to represent? What other examples can be cited from your own experience?

2. What is the meaning of the idea of reading the Bible in one hand and the newspaper in the other? Can you illustrate how this is done by using a recent news item and some pertinent passages from Scripture?

3. What does it mean to you to say that Jesus Christ is "the eschatological reality" of your life?

4. Why is the resurrection regarded by many Christians as the basis for an eschatological faith? What difference would it make if the story of Easter were proved not to be "factual"?

Chapter 2. WHAT IS ESCHATOLOGY?

1. What do you understand now about the meaning of the word "eschatology"? Why do you think that its meaning and connotations have changed during this particular century?

2. Do you think eschatology is necessary for your understanding of what Christian faith is all about, or do

you think it really obscures the main issues? How would you describe gospel without using eschatological content?

3.   Which one of the five eschatological positions that the author discusses seems most convincing to you and why? What are their political implications?

4.   Why do eschatological beliefs seem more important to poor people than to the rich and powerful? Is the attraction of Marxism in the Third World related or not related to your answer?

Chapter 3.   PROPHETS, SEERS, AND RACKETEERS

1.   What do you understand by the terms "apocalyptic," "dispensationalism," and "millennialism"? Why does the author say that what you think of these terms has mainly to do with how you read the Bible?

2.   Would you say that your church is postmillennialist, amillennialist, premillennialist, or takes some other position? What are the reasons for your answer?

3.   What do you think are the comparative dangers and/or helpful advantages to the gospel in millennial preaching? How would you avoid extremes in the doctrine without destroying its essential significance for Christian faith?

4.   What is the relationship between millennial doctrines and the mission of the church?

Chapter 4.   THY KINGDOM COME

1.   What does the petition "Thy kingdom come . . . on earth as it is in heaven" in the Lord's Prayer mean to you? If Jesus brought the Kingdom with him, as some New Testament passages seem to say, why does he ask us to pray for its coming?

2.   What does the author mean by the difference be-

tween the *inaugural* and *eschatological* natures of Jesus' ministry?

3. What sense do you get out of the statement that "the Kingdom is in the midst of the fallen world in both judgment and grace" (p. 59)?

4. What do you understand to be the difference between the conservative and the liberal views on the relation between the world and the Kingdom of God? How do you react to the author's suggestion for a possible synthesis?

Chapter 5. ANOTHER ESCHATOLOGICAL PEOPLE

1. Why and how did the church adapt its earliest eschatological expectations to later conditions in the Roman world?

2. Why does the author say that there are strong eschatological elements in American history? How have these elements been discarded or conserved in more recent times?

3. What were the differences between what the missionaries tried to teach the slaves and what they independently appropriated from the gospel?

4. How does Mbiti say that eschatology in Africa was conditioned by the traditional African religion? How would different concepts of time help or hinder the way people deal with the promise of a better life?

Chapter 6. ESCHATOLOGY IN BLACK

1. What were the three primary responses of the Afro-American slaves to missionary preaching? How were these responses influenced by the residuum of African religion in slave culture?

2. What is the author's argument for accepting what Mbiti says in explaining how eschatology was under-

stood by the slaves, but rejecting Mbiti's idea that the result was necessarily a distortion of the gospel?

3. What is meant by the statement that black spirituality is neither crassly materialistic nor hopelessly other-worldly? How do the spirituals deal with eschatological hope?

4. What does the author understand to be the similarities and differences between black and white Christianity—particularly with reference to eschatology?

Chapter 7. FOLLOWING THE LEADER IN LIFE AND DEATH

1. What do you think about the claim that Christian faith demands our willingness and courage to "follow Jesus" no matter what our instincts and intelligence might tell us?

2. How does eschatology link our daily life and work with the blessings and purposes of God's coming Kingdom? What are some examples from the experience of laity you have known?

3. What is the significance or insignificance of the idea of heaven and hell in formulating one's own approach to Christian eschatology?

4. What is meant by "following Jesus in struggle and celebration"? What aids or prevents this special insight of black faith from being made available to the whole Christian church?

REFERENCES

Chapter 2. WHAT IS ESCHATOLOGY?

Cone, James H. *A Black Theology of Liberation.* J. B. Lippincott Co., 1970.

Moltmann, Jürgen. *The Church in the Power of the Spirit.* Harper & Row, 1977.

Segundo, Juan Luis. "Capitalism Versus Socialism: Crux Theologica," in *Frontiers of Theology in Latin America,* ed. by Rosino Gibellini. Orbis Books, 1979.

Chapter 3. PROPHETS, SEERS, AND RACKETEERS

Cohen, Daniel. *The New Believers: Young Religion in America.* M. Evans and Co., 1975.

Chapter 4. THY KINGDOM COME

Ellul, Jacques. *The Presence of the Kingdom.* Westminster Press, 1951.

Galloway, Allan D. *The Cosmic Christ.* Harper & Brothers, 1951.

Johnson, Joseph A., Jr. *Proclamation Theology.* Fourth Episcopal District Press, 1977.

Chapter 5.   ANOTHER ESCHATOLOGICAL PEOPLE

Mbiti, John S. *New Testament Eschatology in an African Background.* Oxford University Press, 1971.
Petry, Ray C. *Christian Eschatology and Social Thought.* Abingdon Press, 1956.

Chapter 6.   ESCHATOLOGY IN BLACK

Deloria, Vine, Jr. *God Is Red.* Grosset & Dunlap, 1973.
Lovell, John, Jr. *Black Song: The Forge and the Flame.* Macmillan Co., 1972.

Chapter 7.   FOLLOWING THE LEADER IN LIFE
AND DEATH

Du Bois, W. E. B. *The Gift of Black Folk.* 1924; Washington Square Press, 1970.
Moyd, Olin P. *Redemption in Black Theology.* Judson Press, 1979.
Pannenberg, Wolfhart. *Basic Questions in Theology.* Fortress Press, 1970.
Walker, Wyatt Tee. *Somebody's Calling My Name: Black Sacred Music and Social Change.* Judson Press, 1979.
Wilson, Donald C. *Terminal Candor.* Sutter House, 1978.